CARS of the SUPER RICH

THE OPULENT, THE ORIGINAL AND THE OUTRAGEOUS

MARTIN BUCKLEY

MOTORBOOKS
INTERNATIONAL

For Catherine, Sean and Caitlin

This edition first published in 2004 by Motorbooks International, an imprint of
MBI Publishing Company, Galtier Plaza, Suite 200, 380 Jackson Street, St. Paul,
MN 55101-3885 USA

The information in this book is true and complete to the best of our knowledge. All
recommendations are made without any guarantee on the part of the author or Publisher, who
also disclaim any liability incurred in connection with the use of this data or specific details.

We recognize that some words, model names and designations, for example, mentioned herein
are the property of the trademark holder. We use them for identification purposes only. This is
not an official publication.

Motorbooks International titles are also available at discounts in bulk quantity for industrial or
sales-promotional use. For details write to Special Sales Manager at Motorbooks International
Wholesalers & Distributors, Galtier Plaza, Suite 200, 380 Jackson Street,
St. Paul, MN 55101-3885 USA.

Talk to the publisher about this book:
rob@motorbookinternational.co.uk

ISBN 0-7603-1953-7

Printed in China

Cover main image: Ferrari Enzo
Cover inset: Mercedes-Benz CLK GTR
Back cover and title page: Facel Vega Excellence 1957-64
This page: Facel Vega Facel II 1962-64

Contents

Foreword 4

1 Pomp & circumstance 6

2 Exclusivity assured, luxury unlimited 40

3 The jet set 76

4 Rare supercars 96

5 The 200mph club 122

6 Utility cars for the super rich 140

7 The mystique of the 4-door 162

8 Call the taste police 182

Acknowledgements 204

Index 205

Foreword

Cars of the super rich is a sweeping waltz through the most glamorous, expensive and majestic motor cars of the 20th century. It's hard to nail down the precise qualifying elements for inclusion, and no doubt members of enthusiasts' clubs on Route 66 and British devotees of the Ford MkII Granada Ghia X 2.8 injection will be snarling over exclusions.

My apologies. All I can say is I went on gut feeling and embraced those rare, special and bespoke cars in the fields of speed, luxury and ceremonial pomp that have the best stories to tell, and hopefully you won't have heard them before. Most of the big names of top-shelf motoring are included here – along with some others you might not have encountered – but none is above ridicule.

We have attempted to capture the Martini TV commercial chic of a Swiss Monteverdi – and the militaristic utility of a Lamborghini off-roader – as enthusiastically as we wallow in the folklore of some of the world's rarest diplomatic limousines, such as the Hong-Qi Red Flag.

" We have attempted to capture the Martini TV commercial chic of a

Swiss Monteverdi – and the militaristic utility of a Lamborghini off-roader "

Rare, that is the key word here. Rare, special but not necessarily unique or untouchable. There are cars here you may have encountered fleetingly, others that are but distant memories from a faded copy of *World Cars*.

I didn't want to make this a book about show cars and one-offs in the realm of total fantasy but more of an exploration of the most intriguing low volume cars from the 1930s to the present day. From the magisterial magnificence of the doomed 8-litre Bentley to the celebrity-fuelled flash of a Ferrari Enzo, we drive through 70 years of the good, the bad, the ugly and the unforgettable of upmarket motoring, chosen by car lovers as varied as Hollywood superstars and European dictators.

Martin Buckley

January 2004

Pomp &
circumstance

VIP-only limousines are an ignored corner of motoring history but we have assembled some of the rarest and most intriguing. The Bugatti Royale is perhaps the best known, created expressly for royalty but only ever sold to commoners: Ettore Bugatti refused to sell one to King Zog of Albania because he was so appalled by his table manners.

Rolls-Royces are associated with international royalty but Grossers, the biggest and grandest cars from the Mercedes-Benz stable, are symbolic of some of history's dodgiest characters.

America's Lincoln and Cadillac limousines seemed too ubiquitous to feature in this elite company yet they 'inspired' the ZIL (that came equipped with its own bus lanes on the roads of Moscow) and China's Hong-Qi Red Flag. The French, as usual, did things differently: only they could build a sporty state limousine based on an Italian supercar – and get away with it.

Bugatti Royale

NUMBER BUILT : 6

Surely the ultimate luxobarge? The straight-eight, 13-litre Royale was created exclusively for the crowned heads of Europe but none was ever sold to royalty. At least twice the price of the most expensive Rolls-Royce chassis, only six were ever built, but with a 14ft wheelbase and elegant 24in wheels (with integral brake drums), these cars inspired some of the most dramatic and beautiful bodywork ever to grace a motorcar.

Eleven different bodies were built, the fantastic Coupe Napoleon being perhaps the most sensational. Despite their size and 7,000lb weight, Royales are said to be a cinch to drive with light steering and three-speed gearchange. Developing 300bhp at a leisurely 1,700rpm, the engine featured three valves per cylinder, integral main bearings and two plugs per cylinder.

The engine was destined to live beyond the demise of the Royale in 1933 to become a successful railcar engine for the French National Railway. Using two or four Royale engines, 79 Bugatti railcars were built, making this one of Bugatti's greatest financial successes. One established a world average speed record of 122mph.

The huge Bugatti Royale is probably the ultimate collector's car, yet nearly unsaleable when new, and just six were made. Post-war car dealers struggled to raise £300 for a Royale; now they make $16m/£10m at auction. Pic: Giles Chapman Archive

"The Royale was created exclusively for the crowned heads of Europe but none was ever sold to royalty"

"It was a prestigious official sedan for those who were not rich, but a little more equal than others"

Chaika-Gaz 13

NUMBER BUILT: NOT KNOWN

If the ZIL was the Rolls-Royce of Russian cars, then the Chaika (Russian for seagull) was more of the order of a Buick or a British Humber. Like the ZIL, however, it was a prestigious official sedan for those who were not rich, but a little more equal than others. Only the movers and shakers of the Communist Party could drive – or, more likely, be driven in – a Chaika.

Launched in 1958, its shape appeared to be a direct copy of a Packard Caribbean, but it was powered by its own 5.5-litre, 195bhp V8 engine with alloy cylinder heads, and hitched to a push-button three-speed automatic transmission. It was good for 100mph at a time when most other Russian cars struggled to maintain 70, and Chaika occupants could luxuriate in such niceties as powered steering, door locks and window lifts, as well as a five-band radio with automatic antenna. For warmer climes and state occasions, a four-door convertible version was available.

Early Chaikas were offered in upbeat two-tone colour schemes but as the Cold War grew chillier, the car was built only in sombre diplomatic black. Incredibly, production of some models continued into the late 1970s.

The Chaika was built for Soviet goverment officials who were not quite important enough to be driven around in a ZIL. Amazingly this very mid-1950s shape lasted well into the 1970s. Pic: Julian Nowill

Citroen SM Chapron
1972

NUMBER BUILT: 2

For many years, French political leaders used black Citroen DS saloons, some with special bodies built by exclusive national coachbuilders like Henri Chapron and Heuliez. However, they were powered by Maserati V6 engines of only four cylinders and looked a bit under endowed next to Cadillacs and Rollers at diplomatic functions. Thus, the introduction of the Maserati V6-powered Citroen SM in 1970 was a godsend for French national pride. At last France had a luxury supercar to take on the world and the Présidence de la République wasted no time in ordering two long-wheelbase Citroen SM cabriolets. They were delivered in 1972.

They still perform official duties for the Elysée Palace although the last time they were used was in mid-1990s, for a visit by Queen Elizabeth II. They had to be rebuilt specially for the occasion, as inactivity isn't good for their hydropneumatic suspension. Specially modified by the coachbuilder Chapron, they were used extensively by Georges Pompidou and his successor François Mitterrand. The only known technical modification is lower overall gearing for easier slow processional duties (the full-length hood is lowered and raised by hydraulics).

The Citroen connection is maintained today by a much more regularly seen long-wheelbase CX Prestige Turbo in black, which is still used by President Chirac.

"*At last France had a luxury supercar to take on the world*"

*These elegant long wheelbase Citroen SMs by Chapron are still
used at French state occasions. Only two were built, but other
specially adapted SMs were built for rich private owners.*
Pic: Brian Cass

Facel Vega Excellence

NUMBER BUILT: 152

Facel built the Excellence at the behest of the French government which wanted a large, impressive car that would look the part in any diplomatic scenario: the Citroen DS was considered a little commonplace in the most exalted company. Production took a while to get going and there were problems with the doors which had no centre pillar to latch on to and were difficult to keep closed, sometimes opening because of the flexing of the chassis. Not ideal, in a luxury motor. A Chrysler executive, riding in an Excellence in Paris, lost his briefcase which slid across the leather seat onto the road when a door suddenly opened. Passengers enjoyed every luxury imaginable, including some they perhaps couldn't have imagined. Footrests folded down from the backs of the seats and a cosmetics locker in the centre was complete with perfumes, mirror and comb. A radio telephone was just about the only optional extra.

French President Charles de Gaulle could never come to terms with the car because of its American engine but his Interior minister (and his wife) had no such concerns. Various French diplomats used the car as did royalty: the King of Morocco owned an Excellence. Hollywood actress Ava Gardner was an enthusiastic owner of the classy French car and legend has it she ran over a taxi driver while driving it when she was, shall we say, over-refreshed.

"Passengers enjoyed every luxury imaginable,

including some they perhaps couldn't have imagined"

1957-64

The Excellence was not a sucess for Facel which lost money on most of them. There were structural problems with the doors which could open unannounced. Pic: Richard Stevens

Hong-Qi
Red Flag sedan 1958-88

NUMBER BUILT: 1,542

When Chairman Mao visited the Soviet Union in 1949, he rode in ZIL limousines and was impressed. He decided China needed a top people's vehicle and, with help from the Soviets, a factory was opened in 1956. Designers at the new Changchun No1 Automobile Factory fashioned a large, menacing sedan along contemporary North American lines, weighing two tons and powered by an overhead-valve V8 engine based on a Chrysler design.

The prototype was hand-built, and changes were made to give production versions cleaner, more angular lines. The interior featured ivory switches, walnut decoration, tapestry satin seats and all the other refinements expected of a car built for the elite. The trademark of the Red Flag sedan was overlapping red flags representing the components of the proletariat in China – workers, peasants, soldiers, students, intellectuals and businessmen.

Long-wheelbase versions and open-top 'inspection' cars for state occasions were also produced. In the early 1970s Chairman Mao issued instructions for an extra long Hong-Qi to be built, presumably to maintain Chinese dignity on the international stage where the stretched Mercedes 600 was so prominent. A vast limousine, 33ft long, was devised with, curiously, three doors. It was finished in 1976, the year Mao died, and he never had the chance to enjoy it. Hong-Qi Red Flag production continued until 1988 when the Changchun factory switched over to the production of a car based on the Audi 100.

Like most communist limousines, the Hong Qi was heavily influenced by 1950s American design. These cars have hardly ever been seen outside China. Pic: China Motor Vehicle Documentation Centre

"*It was finished in 1976, the year Mao died, and he never had the chance to enjoy it*"

Lancia Flaminia

335 'Quirinale'

1961

NUMBER BUILT: 5

Most top Italian politicians (the names change every week, so volatile are their politics) swan about in bullet-proof long-wheelbase Lancia Kappa saloons, or Alfa 166 3-litres. In the 1980s Italy's President, Sandro Pertini, favoured a Maserati Quattroporte saloon and famously upset Enzo Ferrari when he used the car on a visit to Maranello, home of the prancing horse marque. In the 1970s the car of choice had been the Fiat 130 saloon, usually bullet-proofed, following the kidnapping of Aldo Morro.

But on very special state occasions the Quirinale (Italian parliament) dusts off its four magnificent Lancia Flaminia presidential limousines, built specially by Pininfarina for Queen Elizabeth II's visit to Italy in 1961. Pininfarina was informed of the visit only six months beforehand, and built five cars on this chassis, which featured an all-aluminium V6 2.5-litre engine and a rear-mounted gearbox. They had traditional cloth hoods or a special transparent hardtop if it was raining, plus air conditioning, electric windows and an intercom system. The four cars were given special names – Belsito, Belmonte, Belvedere and Belfiore – and a fifth car is said to have been given to the Queen as a gift, although Buckingham Palace claims to know nothing of this. Does a Flaminia presidential lurk somewhere in a lock-up at Buck House?

The Flaminia Quirinale is one of the world's most majestic and important-looking state vehicles. Here is an important Italian person using the car as intended. Pic: Pininfarina Archive

Mercedes-Benz Grosser
1930-40

NUMBER BUILT: APPROX 200

The Grosser Mercedes was built specifically with heads of state in mind – users included German Emperor Kaiser Wilhelm II (who died the year after production ceased), Adolf Hitler and Emperor Hirohito of Japan. It might not be an aspect of its history Mercedes would like us to dwell on but Daimler-Benz cars were among Hitler's favourites and played their part in his rise to power.

Mercedes-Benz automobiles were seen as symbols of the prosperous Germany promised by the Nazis, and were often displayed by party leaders. These vast 7.6-litre, eight-cylinder Grosser limousines, with open or closed bodywork, were fast and strong allowing Hitler and his top associates to campaign throughout Germany at a speed that caught his political opponents napping.

State power brought almost infinite resources into the hands of the Nazi Party, and liberal use of luxury Mercedes limousines was a perk of the job. Hitler enjoyed cars, and his armoured, five-ton 777K supercharged limousine was good for 100mph on 200bhp but returned only 9-10mpg. Hitler's Grosser Mercedes 777W 150 can be seen at the Canadian War Museum in Ottawa.

Grosser owners tended to leave the driving to a man in a peaked cap – this model is the 1930-37 type with Sedanca bodywork. Pic: DaimerlerChrysler Archive

"*Daimler-Benz cars were among Hitler's favourites*

and played their part in his rise to power"

Mercedes 600 Pullman

"*Curiously, the German government didn't own any 600s but were lent them by Mercedes*"

1963-80

NUMBER BUILT: 487

If Hitler were still alive, he'd still want to be driven around in a Mercedes 600 Pullman. From the 1960s right through to the 70s and 80s, this 6.3-litre, 130mph air-suspended powered-everything super-limo was the ultimate dictator's car. It was favoured by despots of all political colours (they liked it because it didn't have the Imperialist connotations of a Rolls or a Cadillac), as well as by most of Germany's chancellors. Chairman Mao is said to have had 23 of them and Uganda's late dictator, Idi Amin, owned three. World leaders past and present including Japan's Emperor Hirohito, President Tito of Yugoslavia and Egypt's President Mubarak have ridden around in them, alongside European royalty and Pope John Paul II.

Curiously, the German government didn't own any 600s but were lent them by Mercedes who retained a fleet to be used as required. Today a 600 Landaulette (open-top) is still used for special state functions but you are more likely to see Gerhard Schroeder, the current Germany Chancellor, in the back of an Audi A8, a Mercedes S-Class or BMW 7 Series.

The car in the main picture is a short-wheelbase 600 Landaulette built for a special customer. The interior shots highlight the luxury enjoyed by VIPs in the 600 class yet with none of the vulgarity of an American limousine. Pic: DaimlerChrysler Archive

Rolls-Royce Phantom

NUMBER BUILT: 18

Before her coronation as Queen Elizabeth, the young Princess Elizabeth – encouraged by the Duke of Edinburgh – bought the first in a long line of Rolls-Royces in 1950. It was a Phantom IV, a massive eight-cylinder limousine built to special order for royalty and international heads of state. Other owners would include her sister Princess Margaret, Spain's fascist leader General Franco (he chose a 1952 Mulliner-bodied armour-plated cabriolet) and several Arab royals, such as Prince Talal al Saoud of Saudi Arabia who used a Franay-bodied model. The production run was 18 and all but one – the Shah of Iran's limousine – survive.

The Queen's own model was fitted with a specially modified driver's seat in case the Duke of Edinburgh – a keen MG TC sports car owner in his bachelor days – wished to drive the 100mph Phantom IV.

It ran without number plates and was fitted with the usual blue light and royal standard (like all British state cars). The Phantom IV was the royal family's official state limousine and carried the Queen to the opening of Parliament in 1954. It remains in perfect condition in the Royal Mews and is still occasionally used on official business.

The Phantom IV had a straight-eight engine and was built strictly for royalty and other heads of state. This car is still in the Royal Mews in perfect condition . Pic: Classic Cars

"The Queen's own model was fitted with a specially modified driver's seat in case the Duke of Edinburgh wished to drive the 100mph Phantom IV"

IV

Rolls-Royce

The Phantom V and Phantom VI were perhaps the last truly imposing limousines before the trend towards stretched standard sedans took over entirely. Pic Frank Dale & Stepsons

"The Park Ward Landaulette was for royalty and heads of state only"

Phantom VI
Landaulette 1968-90

NUMBER BUILT: 12

The Phantom VI was the last Rolls-Royce to have a separate chassis and non-independent rear suspension and had drum brakes until the end of production in 1990. It was constructed specifically to be fitted with coachbuilt seven-passenger limousine bodywork of the most formal kind and all but a handful came with an HJ Mulliner Park Ward design, built in alloy at their factory in north-west London.

The first Phantom VI limousines were built in 1968 but the model was merely a derivative of the Phantom V, announced in 1959. Mechanically and structurally this car was a stretched Silver Cloud II with the latest 6.2-litre V8 engine fitted, allowing a top speed of well over 100mph. It was finally ousted from production by modern legislation.

Although Rolls-Royce would sell a Phantom to anybody with sufficient funds. the Park Ward Landaulette was for royalty and heads of state only. They built one for the Queen Mother and various Arab royals.

The Queen has had two special Phantoms built for her. The first, Canberra, was delivered in 1960 with a special raised roofline featuring a large perspex panel over the rear part of the roof. A second car in the Canberra style was delivered (months late due to strikes) as a present from the UK's Society of Motor Manufacturers and Traders for the Silver Jubilee in 1977. These cars are still in use.

Tatra 613 Limousine

NUMBER BUILT: UNKNOWN

R ear-engined cars were few and far between by the mid-Seventies yet Tatra, cut off from the rest of the world in communist Czechoslovakia, was committed to the layout. So when the new 613 saloon appeared nobody was shocked to find its engine in the tail. Aware of the handling problems associated with tail-heavy cars, this new four-cam air-cooled unit was moved much further forward compared with the old 603, to a point ahead of the rear axle line in the chassis.

For state and diplomatic use Tatra assembled five-metre-wheelbase limousine versions of the 613, some with Laundaulette bodywork. Unlike the 'standard' versions these long wheelbase cars had automatic transmission.

These were swift, quiet cars built in small numbers as a sideline to Tatra's truck business. Following the fall of communism, Tatra's future was always under threat from the influx of prestige European marques, despite two attempts at bringing the 613 up to date. Post Communism, the new Czech government eschewed Tatra as being too closely associated with the old order and replaced their 613s with the inevitable Mercedes. Tatra car production ended in 1998.

Czech diplomats and other VIPs now travel by S-Class Mercedes but in the 1970s this long-wheelbase Tatra 613 was the height of their aspirations Pic: Julian Nowill

"Following the fall of communism, Tatra's future was always under threat from the influx of prestige European marques"

ZIL 111, 111A & 111V
1958-68

NUMBER BUILT: UNKNOWN

Even when the USSR was at odds with the USA during the Cold War, American automobile design had a strong influence on the big cars used to transport political leaders around Moscow and the rest of the country. The ZIS (Zavod Imieni Stalina) was a favourite but had to be renamed when the memory of Stalin fell out of favour. It became the ZIL, though the 'L' stood for Ligachev rather than Lenin. Yegor Kuzmich Ligachev was a high-ranking Communist Party official who rose to prominence during the leadership of Mikhail Gorbachev though he disagreed with many of his boss's economic reform plans. Three modern American cars had been purchased for evaluation before design of the ZIL began, and Packard was the favoured marque, as it had been when planning the ZIS.

The styling of the first ZIL was clearly influenced by the 1950s Packard Caribbean: it was powered by a 6-litre 200bhp V8 engine and featured a push-button automatic transmission (clearly American inspired). The 111 was the standard ZIL and the 111A was a stretched version that was more than 20ft long. The car weighed in at 6,200lb but could top 100mph. For special occasions there was the 111V with an open body and an electric hood. ZIL drivers enjoyed power steering, electric windows and air conditioning. The drivers and their VIP passengers (mainly members of the politburo) did not have to endure traffic jams as the cars used 'ZIL-only lanes' in Moscow. The 111 had a minor restyle in 1962 that featured a Cadillac-inspired quad-headlamp front end.

ZIL 111 in a suitably chilly setting. The biggest, fastest cars in Russia were invariably painted black and were an imposing sight as they travelled down 'ZIL lanes' on Moscow's wide boulevards. Pic: Julian Nowill

"*The ZIS was a favourite but had to be renamed when the memory of Stalin fell out of favour*"

ZIL 114-117 & 4014
1967 – to date

NUMBER BUILT: UNKNOWN

The ZIL 114 replaced the 111 as Russia's top car in 1967. Despite a new lightweight aluminium engine, it was even heavier at 6,720lb but the engine's 300bhp could waft up to 118mph, drinking deeply from its 26-gallon fuel tank. ZILs had a relatively high 9.5:1 compression ratio and required special fuel. The body shape was again American inspired, possibly with leanings towards the big Chryslers and Imperials of the mid-1960s. The ZIL 114 had disc brakes on all wheels and twin batteries were required for the various power assists inside. To supplement the 114 a shorter, lighter 117 version of the ZIL became available in 1971 and was the first Russian passenger car to exceed 125mph.

The current 41041 ZIL, announced in 1978, had a gaudy restyle with an imitation Mercedes front grille. Powered by an even bigger 7695cc V8 it weighed 7300lbs in seven-seater form but a smaller five-seater was available, as well as a convertible. The ZIL continues to be built in the same truck factory and Russian leaders still use them: Russian president Vladimir Putin took two with him when he visited Britain.

Former Soviet president Mikhail Gorbachev was allowed to keep his ZIL after he was ousted from power until his successor, Boris Yeltsin, decided he was being too critical of the new regime and took the car away, replacing it with three downmarket Volgas.

The later 114 series ZIL had even more brutal styling – cast in the mould of contemporary Cadillacs and Mercedes. Hardly beautiful but very intimidating. Pic: Julian Nowill

" The ZIL continues to be built in the same truck factory and Russian leaders still use them "

BMW 505 1955

"The Chancellor knocked his hat off while climbing into the rear of the car ... and at that moment the 505 lost its chance of becoming a rival to the big Mercedes"

NUMBER BUILT: 3

BMW was jealous of Mercedes' domination of the state limousine business in the 1950s and tried to tempt Chancellor Konrad Adenauer out of his 300 limousine with a long wheelbase version of its 502 saloon, called 505. The big Mercedes 300 cars had become so synonymous with the German politician that even to this day, the nickname of the car is 'Adenauer 300', so as not to confuse it with later 300-badged Mercedes.

Styled by Giovanni Michelotti of Italy, and built by Ghia-Aigle of Switzerland, the BMW 505 was longer and taller than the standard saloon and had all the luxuries expected of such a vehicle including a central partition and air conditioning. Its dimensioned aped those of the Mercedes 300 and the styling even flattered the Stuttgart car somewhat by imitating its tall greenhouse look and rear wing line. However, the story goes that the Chancellor knocked his hat off while climbing into the rear of the car in front of a group of tense BMW executives, and at that moment the 505 lost its chance of becoming a rival to the big Mercedes on the State limousine fleet.

Of the original two cars, one was retained by BMW for state visits to the factory and the second was sold. BMW built a third in-house in 1963.

The unlucky BMW 505 was BMW's attempt to build a diplomatic limousine for German VIPs and steal some of Mercedes' thunder. Just three were built. Pic: BMW Historic Archive

Tatra T600 Cabrio

NUMBER BUILT: 1

Post 1945, Tatra found itself behind the Iron Curtain under the centralised planned economy forced on Czechoslovakia by its new Russian masters. Hans Ledwinka, Tatra's chief engineer, was thrown in jail by the communists for allegedly collaborating with the Nazis and on his release returned to his native Austria. There was little sign of a car for the super rich. The first car designed under the new regime was the T600 Tatraplan, the name a reference to the centralised planned economy.

The cars were built almost exclusively for Communist Party members and senior Czech officials or industry leaders. It was still rear-engined but instead of an air-cooled V8, there was a horizontally-opposed 'four'. Several thousand of the four-door saloons were built with characteristic aerodynamic styling. Several thousand of the standard saloon versions were assembled and exported widely but Tatra also sanctioned occasional specials like the Monte Carlo (fitted with a V8 engine) which was the fastest car in Czechoslovakia at the time. However, the most famous T600 special was the aluminium-bodied T600 Cabrio built as a 70th birthday present for Russian leader Joseph Stalin in 1949 and displayed at the Geneva motor show that year. The body was constructed by local coachbuilders Sodomka.

This not unattractive Tatra T600 Cabrio was built specially for Joe Stalin's birthday in an attempt to get into his good books. Standard T600s can be seen under construction in the background. Pic: Classic Cars

"*As the Japanese motor industry grew and prospered, the Prince Royal was a symbol of its independence and confidence*"

Nissan Prince

Royal Limousine

NUMBER BUILT: 6

The Prince Royal was the first VIP limousine built in Japan. It was exclusively for the Japanese Royal Family, who had previously used large limousines from other nations. As the Japanese motor industry grew and prospered, the Prince Royal was a symbol of its independence and confidence. The first Prince cars appeared in 1952, named after Crown Prince Akihito, and after the company became a division of Nissan in the early 1960s its Skyline and Gloria models became the basis of Nissan's big car range. Launched at the Tokyo motor show in 1966, the Prince Royal was a vast car of restrained, handsome appearance, its long wheelbase giving room for a driver and seven passengers. The driver's seat was leather but the VIP passengers, who were behind a screen, sat on wool cloth, enjoying air conditioning and possibly some drinks from the wine box as they cruised up to 100mph. The Japanese Royals could speak to the driver on an intercom. The car was propelled by a 6.4-litre V8 engine that was probably related to the smaller Nissan President engine. For parades, when the engine might overheat, there was a bigger radiator with twin fans. The Prince Royal had highly traditional suspension arrangements with a beam rear axle, leaf springs and drum brakes all round. Nisssan is thought to have built six of these cars and all are still owned by the Japanese Imperial family.

The sober lines of the Nissan Prince Royal don't look Japanese
and may have been the work of Italy's Pininfarina which did
much behind-the-scenes design for Nissan in the 1960s.
Picture: courtesy of the Japanese Imperial Family

Exclusivity assured, luxury unlimited

The Duesenberg, Rolls-Royce Phantom III, 8-litre Bentley and the Aston Martin V12 Lagonda epitomised luxury, power and exclusivity immediately before and after World War II. Austerity, commercial pressures and the development of monoccque construction may have somewhat curtailed the activities of the coachbuilder post-1945 yet there remained a steady demand from those who demanded exclusivity regardless of price. Britain's Daimler 'Green Goddess' straight-eight was unimaginably decadent and succeeded on its own terms where over-ambitious newcomers like the Isotta Fraschini Monterosa and Invicta Black Prince failed. Chrysler and Ghia formed an alliance in the 1950s to build spectacularly glamorous special-order cars exclusively for rat-packers and Arab royalty. As car makers chased the wallets of the rich in the 1950s, Cadillac lost money on every Eldorado Brougham it built, but somehow that wasn't the point. In America, the most outrageously expensive and exclusive production Lincoln is still the Continental II.

Bentley 8-litre

1931

NUMBER BUILT: 100

The 8-litre was W O Bentley's attempt to wrest the title of 'best car in the world' from Rolls-Royce. It was unfortunate for him that his 200bhp, 100mph flagship made its debut in the midst of a world recession. Only 100 chassis were laid down before company backer Woolf Barnato pulled the purse strings and put the company into receivership.

Rolls-Royce took over in 1931 and one of its first acts was to kill off the magnificent 8-litre, one of the few cars that could challenge its Phantom. Although previous Bentleys had sporting overtones (the company had won the 24-hour Le Mans race five times) the 8-litre was intended to be a fast and effortless luxury carriage that more often than not carried sober saloon bodywork. Even in this form it could easily reach 100mph – torque from the imposingly long six-cylinder overhead camshaft engine was never disclosed but it must have been huge – and the 8-litre, if anything, was more manageable to handle that its predecessors. Too many of these fabulous cars have lost their original bodywork in favour of replica open-tourers, but the survival rate of the 8-litre is high.

"Too many of these fabulous cars have lost their original bodywork in favour of replica open-tourers"

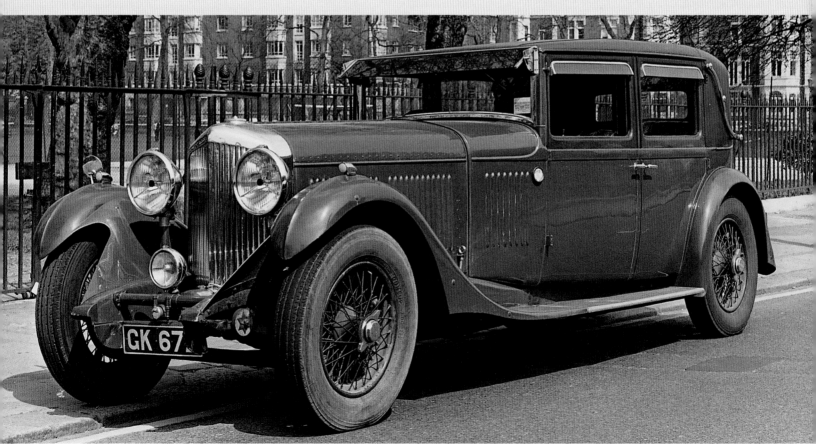

Bentley Cresta

NUMBER BUILT: 17

The Bentley Cresta was conceived by Facel Vega boss Jean Daninos, a long-time Bentley owner looking for a more sporting car for his own use. The Cresta had a lower radiator header tank and scuttle, and a shorter, more raked steering column. A higher (3.42:1) final drive ratio hinted at the car's high-speed ambitions.

Italian stylist Pininfarina built a rakish two-door, four-seater coupe in steel and aluminium, dispensing with the traditional grille in favour of a low, wide design that caused ructions in the Bentley boardroom when displayed at the Paris motor show in 1948. Daninos told his body builders to modify the radiator design to something Bentley found more edifying. Daninos claimed to have bodied 17 cars, marketed under the brand Cresta – the name Bentley used on its prototype chassis before the war. The cars were built in workshops separate from mainstream Facel production until 1950 and sold to an international clientele including Prince Rainier of Monaco, French heart-throb actor Yves Montand and Giovanni Agnelli of Fiat. Daninos bought the final chassis in January 1951 and fashioned on it a coupe of his own design called Cresta II.

The slimmer, more powerful look (the Farina shape was rather bloated) incorporated the trend-setting, vertically stacked headlights and 'nostrils' either side of the front grille that anticipated the look of the Facel Vega three years before its debut.

The final Bentley Cresta was this svelte design that predicted the shape of future Facel Vega models. It was built especially for the wife of Facel boss Jean Daninos. Pic: Richard Stevens

"The slimmer, more powerful look ...

anticipated the Facel Vega three years before its debut "

Crown Imperial
Ghia Limousines 1957–64

NUMBER BUILT: 95

Imperial was Chrysler Corporation's upmarket brand created to compete directly with Cadillac and Lincoln. For much of the 1950s, its cars had rather sedate styling but after 1954, Imperial became a separate division and things began to change.

Since the early 1950s, there had been a close association with coachbuilders Ghia of Turin who produced many of Chrysler's show cars and prototypes. In 1954, Imperial built a special limousine for Pope Pius XII on a Chrysler Imperial chassis. Chrysler wanted to offer a hand-crafted, premium-price limousine to challenge Cadillac's dominance but without the tooling costs of a new body.

The answer lay with Ghia which assembled such a car one at a time much more cheaply than Chrysler could in America. Chrysler did the styling in-house and shipped a kit of mechanical parts to Ghia whose staff lengthened the car and then hand-built the body to a high standard, spending two days fitting the doors.

Each eight-passenger Imperial limousine took sixth months from order to delivery. The car sold for nearly three times the price of an ordinary Imperial, attracting orders from New York Governor Nelson Rockefeller, Lyndon B Johnson (who became US President in 1963 following the assassination of John F Kennedy) and comedy legend Jack Benny.

"Chrysler wanted to offer a hand-crafted, premium-price

limousine to challenge Cadillac's dominance"

The straight-eight engine of the 'Green Goddess' meant the body had cartoon-like proportions, low slung with a massive bonnet. Pic: Frank Dale and Stepsons

"*American author Clive Cussler, who owns one of the eight cars, has immortalised it in his Dirk Pitt private eye series as the car driven by his literary hero*"

Daimler Straight-eight 'Green Goddess' 1948-51

NUMBER BUILT: 8

The Hooper-bodied straight-eight drophead coupe was one of the most ostentatious cars built by Daimler. It was known as the 'Green Godddess' because of its pastel jade green coachwork, and was the most expensive car on display when making its debut at the 1948 London Motor Show.

Twenty feet long, and 6ft 5in wide, this dramatic four-seater drop-head had a hood that folded away under a metal cover behind the rear seats (the whole procedure was powered).

The windows were raised and lowered electrically and the front screen was so wide it needed three windscreen wipers. The front bench seat could seat three and there were armchair seats in the rear for two. The front lights are faired in behind Perspex covers (some of the other cars at the show had more conventional lights). A hand-washer was built in to the wheel-changing equipment.

American author Clive Cussler, who owns one of the eight cars, has immortalised it as the car driven by his literary hero, the private detective Dirk Pitt.

Duesenberg SJ

1932-37

NUMBER BUILT: 26

European enthusiasts often deride post World War II American cars but the 1930s Duesenberg SJ was as good as any in the world. The coachwork was spectacular but the SJ of 1929 was more than just a pretty face: in supercharged form, its twin-cam, four-valves-per-cylinder Lycoming straight-eight engine produced 320bhp and could push the monstrous car up to 130mph. With its hemispherical combustion chambers, fully balanced five-bearing nickel-plated crankshaft, this long-stroke design could rev safely to 5000rpm. There were servo-assisted hydraulic brakes to slow down the SJ, which had a massive chassis with six tubular cross members.

In chassis form alone, the car was more expensive than a Rolls-Royce and ownership was strictly the preserve of millionaires and film stars: Clark Gable, Gary Cooper, Greta Garbo and William Randolph Hurst all owned SJs.

Founded in 1920 by Fred and August Duesenberg, the company was best known for its racing cars but poor sales led to a takeover by E.L. Cord at the end of the decade. Cord gave the brothers the money to build the ultimate car from scratch, the J and SJ being the result. Only 26 SJs were built between 1932 and the end of production in 1937.

The Duesenberg SJ was perhaps the ultimate pre-war American supercar with a client base that was almost entirely Hollywood A-list. Pic Giles Chapman Archive

"*The car was more expensive than a Rolls-Royce and ownership
was strictly the preserve of film millionaires and film stars*"

Cadillac Eldorado Brougham 1957-58

NUMBER BUILT: 704

The 1957 Eldorado Brougham, the most prestigious Cadillac since the V16 models of 17 years earlier, was GM's answer to Ford's Continental II. It started life as a design exercise and the pillarless styling and knife-edge fins were almost restrained for this gaudy period in American design. Quad headlights, a stainless steel roof and narrow-band whitewall tyres were industry firsts.

The advanced air-suspension system, with self-levelling valves and a small engine-driven compressor, was notoriously unreliable. Powered by Cadillac's 6.3-litre V8, the Brougham was marketed as a super-exclusive model for the super-rich (Frank Sinatra drove one) and featured an amazing list of standard features unmatched at the time. Power steering, power brakes and automatic transmission were becoming the norm on cars of this class but the Brougham was also fitted with an automatic headlamp dipper, cruise control, electric door locks, memory seats and an electric bootlid opener. There were magnetised drinks tumblers in the glove box, cigarette and tissue dispensers and a cosmetics set that included lipstick, powder puff, mirror and comb and an Arpege atomiser with Lanvin perfume. Cadillac offered 44 trim combinations and couldn't sell the Brougham for anything like the build-cost and after two years of losses the model was dropped.

This Cadillac promotional shot mixes fins and all-American womanhood. With its complex electrical system and air suspension, it was one of the most expensive Cadillacs ever built. Pic: Classic Cars

"*Cadillac offered 44 trim combinations and couldn't sell the Brougham for anything like the build-cost*"

> *"The Brougham was almost twice the price of the next most expensive '59 Cadillac, the glamorous and famously finned Biarritz convertible"*

Cadillac's close association with Pininfarina in the 1950s and early 60s produced beautiful cars like this Jacqueline Coupe with no hint of a fin. Pic: Giles Chapman Archive

Cadillac

Eldorado Brougham
Jacqueline Coupé 1959

NUMBER BUILT: 99

Two years after the launch of the first Eldorado Brougham, Cadillac introduced a replacement, which was the ultimate in American luxury: unimaginably sybaritic, incredibly expensive and very rare. Only 99 were handbuilt by Pininfarina in Italy. At $13,000/£4,600 the Brougham was almost twice the price of the next most expensive '59 Cadillac, the glamorous and famously finned Biarritz convertible.

The Biarritz represented the summit of the tail fin and the Brougham quietly ushered in a new era of leaner, cleaner styling that would become the Cadillac look in the 1960s. Glitz and vulgarity were slowly giving way to crisp-edged restraint. The original 1957 Brougham was an incredible cost-no-object exercise with every luxury imaginable: each car sold lost $10,000/£3,500 for Cadillac.

The next Brougham had to be just as exclusive, just as luxurious, just as rare – but cheaper to build and Cadillac needed an outside company better able to deal with small volumes.

Pininfarina agreed to hand-build 100 Broughams a year but one chassis slipped its crate, so the story goes, and dropped in the harbour at Detroit. This probably explains why Pininfarina made up the numbers by building 101 cars for the 1960 model year. The Brougham was the last Pininfarina Cadillac until the Allante of the 1980s although the beautiful Brougham-based Jacqueline Coupe show car (named after Jacqueline Kennedy) was almost certainly a sales pitch by Pininfarina for another contract.

Invicta Black Prince

1946-50

NUMBER BUILT: 25

This was a hugely ambitious luxury car project from a British company that had built fast and much respected touring cars in the 1930s. The sinister-sounding Black Prince was powered by a 120bhp straight-six, double overhead camshaft engine, with twin spark plugs per cylinder, triple carbs and a 24-volt electric system. The hefty chassis featured independent torsion bar springing all round and an early form of CVT (continuously variable transmission) called 'hydro kinetic turbo transmitter'. This sounded marvellous but proved almost impossible to get into reverse: most of the surviving cars now have Jaguar manual gearboxes.

The technology was just too ambitious and as it was 10 times the price of a Ford Anglia (a popular car of the day) the Black Prince found only 25 takers. Some were built with sleek saloon bodywork while others were slightly prosaic-looking drophead coupes. AFN, builders of the Frazer Nash, took over the assets of Invicta in 1950.

This Black Prince was marooned in its owner's garden for many years because he couldn't get it into reverse gear. Pic: Giles Chapman Archive

"The transmission, called hydro kinetic turbo transmitter, sounded

marvellous but the car proved almost impossible to get into reverse"

"*Created to generate work for the company after its contracts*

to produce engines for planes and trucks in World War II ended"

Isotta Fraschini

Monterosa

NUMBER BUILT: 4

The Isotta Fraschini Monterosa was one of the great lost causes of the Italian motor industry. This vast 8-cylinder, rear-engined luxury car was created to generate work for the company after its contracts to produce engines for planes and trucks in World War II ended with a return to peace.

Isotta had not produced passenger vehicles since the early 1930s but its straight-eight luxury cars still had a fine reputation. Influenced by the contemporary Tatra, the 3.4-litre V8 engine of the Monterosa was mounted well to the rear of the box section chassis but, unlike the Czech car, it was water cooled with a front-mounted radiator. With swing axles at the back the handling must have had a certain frisson to it. The engine was an early project of the young Aurelio Lampredi who would later go on to great things with Ferrari and Fiat.

Four cars were built before the company ceased trading in 1949, closed by its owners, the Italian government. These were a four-door Berlina by Rapi (built by Zagato), another four-door Berlina (by Touring), a two-door Berlina (also by Touring) and a cabriolet (by Boneschi).

The voluptuous Monterosa was not the car to tempt post-war tycoons out of their Rolls-Royces and Cadillacs but was an intriguing piece of technology. Pic: Giles Chapman Archive

Lagonda V12

NUMBER BUILT: 189

Only 189 Lagonda V12s were built over two years, with production shortened by the outbreak of World War II. Clothed in some of the most beautiful bodywork ever seen on a British chassis – mostly the inspiration of in-house stylist Frank Feeley – they represented the ultimate in high-powered English luxury exotica in the late 1930s.

The car marked a renaissance in the fortunes of W.O. Bentley, the engineer who created it, because he had been sidelined when the company was absorbed by Rolls-Royce in 1931.

W.O. eagerly accepted the job of chief engineer offered by Lagonda's new owner, Alan Good, in 1935. Work on the V12 – Lagonda's bid to build 'the best car in the world' – started shortly afterwards and W.O. was perfectly placed to wreak revenge on his old masters.

The car that made a last minute appearance at the 1936 London Motor Show had an engine made of wood but three complete cars were shown at the following year's show. With its overhead camshafts and an ability to rev to 5,500rpm or more, an output of 200bhp was planned but the production 4.5-litre V12 Lagonda gave around 160bhp. This was enough to power two tons of luxurious arrogance at more than 105mph, making the V12 Lagonda one of the fastest cars on the road. It was wonderfully smooth but proved difficult to service.

The troubled Lagonda V12 was probably the best and most elegant car the company ever built. Pic: Frank Dale & Stepson

"The car that made a last minute appearance at the

1936 London Motor Show had an engine made of wood"

" *Dealers were under instructions not to allow gangsters or other undesirables to buy one* **"**

Elvis Presley looks mean and moody with his Continental II. Dealers were under orders not to sell the cars to hoodlums or other undesirables. Pic: Pictorial Press

Lincoln
Continental II 1956-57

NUMBER BUILT: 2,994

The Continental II was Lincoln's attempt to move even further upmarket with an ultimate luxury car. Stepping aside from the vulgarity of most of Detroit's mid-1950s products, the Continental II had almost European styling and simple detailing, although it was built on the same massive scale as its contemporaries, measuring 18 feet.

The car was virtually hand-built, with endless layers of paint, and Lincoln tested the power output of each engine. The company produced an average of 13 Continentals a day and the cars were shipped in a special fleece-lined canvas cover to avoid any chance of damage to the paintwork.

To protect the car's image, specially selected dealers were expected to sell the Continental to the right kind of customer ... they were under instructions not to allow gangsters or other undesirables to buy one. The Continental II appealed to big-name celebrities and owners included Elvis Presley and Frank Sinatra.

Even with a list price of $10,000/£3,500, buyers jostled for position in the order queue and some cars were sold for as much as $1,000/£350 over list. It wasn't to last though: the Mk II was a money-loser for Ford (which owned Lincoln) and there simply were not enough buyers with requisite cash (Rolls-Royces came cheaper). The classy Continental II lasted just a couple of seasons and was dropped to make way for a much more expensive failure – the Edsel.

Mercedes 540K Special

NUMBER BUILT: 6

Many 540Ks (K for Kompressor) were frumpy tourers and saloons but Mercedes-Benz built six with flamboyant special roadster bodywork. The Special Roadster was a 17ft two-seater with a long tail, and bordered on the camp.

The Roadster was a fabulously well-built car – only Stuttgart's best operatives were used to produce them – with squeezed air and howling supercharged engines making a noise to thrill every 1930s schoolboy.

There was fairly modest 115bhp performance with the supercharger idle but a kick on the throttle brought in the full 180bhp, launching the car down one of Hitler's new autobahns at 106mph. It would cruise at 90mph when most cars wouldn't maintain 60. Driven gently, the straight-eight 5401cc engine might give 8mpg but for those who could afford twice the price of a V16 Cadillac, that probably didn't matter. Ideal transport for movie moguls (famously Jack Warner) and Indian maharajas (one used his 540K to chase tigers), the appearance of a 540K Special Roadster at auction is a major event.

Special K: the most glamorous roadster of the 1930s and a symbol of Teutonic excellence for men in full-length leather jackets. Pic: DaimlerChrysler Archive

"The Special Roadster was a 17ft two-seater with a long tail, and bordered on the camp"

Roadster 1936–1939

Rolls-Royce Phantom

NUMBER BUILT: 710

The Phantom III was a new and more sophisticated type of Rolls-Royce, powered not by the traditional in-line six but a 7338cc V12. It featured twin distributors, dual coils and 24 spark plugs: cutting edge stuff in 1935. On an estimated 160bhp, it was silent at 90mph. It was the first Rolls-Royce with independent front suspension and featured speed sensitive dampers that were automatically adjusted by a pump driven off the four-speed gearbox.

The Phantom III was easily the most expensive Rolls-Royce and that was before you ordered bodywork from the likes of Mulliners, Hoopers, Barkers or one of half a dozen other approved coachbuilders to the gentry.

For all its sophistication, the Phantom III was a relative failure. There was talk of technical problems with the hydraulic tappets and the cooling system, which put buyers off. Sales were evaporating by 1938 and even if the war hadn't intervened, it seems certain that the Phantom III would have been axed by 1940. During hostilities the cars were almost made extinct when the British government considered requisitioning all the cars for their engines, which made ideal glider-launching units, but the idea was dropped. Poor storage during the war years highlighted engine snags and many examples were sold for scrap. Some where even converted to diesel power ...ugh.

The Phantom III was perfect transport for affluent surgeons, lawyers and businessmen, but it was also another troubled pre-war British V12 luxury car. Pic: Frank Dale & Stepsons

> "*Poor storage during the war years highlighted engine snags and many examples were sold for scrap*"

"*The Zeppelin was so hefty, drivers needed a heavy goods licence before they could take to take the wheel*"

Maybach DS-8

Zeppelin 1931-40

NUMBER BUILT: APPROX 215

It's no accident that Mercedes chose to name its new 'ultimate saloon' Maybach, for its pre-war namesake was a truly awesome car. Weighing in at up to three tons – some of the coachwork was exceptionally grandiose – these mammoth cars were powered by an 8-litre, side-valve V12 engine giving 200bhp and 118mph through eight forward speeds and four reverse.

There was a choice of ratios from a 14:1 bottom gear to 2.5:1 in overdrive top and they used vacuum operation with two small levers on the steering wheel. The Zeppelin was so hefty, drivers needed a heavy goods licence before they could take to the wheel. Under the 7ft-long bonnet was an engine derived from the units that powered Graf Zeppelin airships, which were built at the same works as the cars. Coachwork ranged from modest, restrained open tourers to dramatic cabriolets. Spohn of Ravensburg produced some of the best-looking coachwork but all Zeppelins were majestic cars with a dominant presence that made them popular with celebrities, church leaders and statesmen alike. The aerodynamicist Paul Jaray devised a quite hideous streamliner – spare wheels and fitted luggage were concealed in the bulbous front wings.

The 1930s Maybach Zeppelin was flamboyant in styling,
awesome in size and extremely fast, with an 8-litre engine
that made a personal contribution to global warming.
Pic: DaimlerChrysler Archive

Chrysler Ghia L 6.4

1960-62

NUMBER BUILT: 26

Many Italian design studies were based on American production cars in the 1950s and 60s but few made it beyond the stage of one-off prototype. One exception was the Ghia L 6.4 of 1960, and 26 were built in two years.

It was a big coupe, inspired by the Ghia Dart designed by Virgil Exner, who in 1949 became Chrysler Corporation's first styling vice president. He once said car design was 'art made practical'.

The Ghia L 6.4 bore a striking resemblance to Fiat's 2300S Coupe, another Ghia design of the period. Hand-built, and based on Chrysler's 6.4-litre V8, the L 6.4's $15,000/£5,350 price tag meant it was within reach only of the very rich and its exclusiveness gave it tremendous appeal to stars like Frank Sinatra, Dean Martin and their Rat Pack friends.

The L 6.4 was funded by Gene Casaroll of Automobile Shippers Inc who had initiated a similar project in the 1950s which inspired the Dodge Firearrow (102 of those cars were built). The L 6.4 was much less successful: 26 found owners.

Frank Sinatra was a great enthusiast of Ghia-bodied Chryslers which were also sold to other members of the Hollywood star Rat Pack. Pic: Pictorial Press

"Its exclusiveness gave it tremendous appeal to stars like

Frank Sinatra, Dean Martin and their Rat Pack friends"

Glas V8 1965-67

NUMBER BUILT: 271

Hans Glas got into the car business with the Goggomobile in the 1950s and its main contribution to automotive engineering was the pioneering use of the toothed-belt camshaft drive (rather than a chain), which virtually every manufacturer would adopt in the following years. Glas cars became increasingly ambitious until, by 1963, the German company was challenging BMW in the mid-range 1.5-litre class with the 1700 Saloon.

Glas didn't stop there. As a flagship to outdo the Bavarians, Glas introduced an exotic 2.6-litre V8 coupe in 1965, styled and built by Frua of Italy. Germans christened this 121mph flagship the 'Glaserati' and it had its own V8 engine (two Glas four-cylinder units sharing a crankshaft). It was pitched in price midway between the Porsche 911 and 912 and should have done well; but Glas was losing money on all its cars (apart from the miniature Goggomobile) because its range was too diverse. Money problems forced Glas to allow a takeover by BMW in 1966 but the V8 survived briefly to become the BMW-Glas 3000, with a stroked version of the overhead camshaft engine. BMW wanted the Glas factory at Dingolfing, near Munich, for its own activities and shut down production of the beautiful V8 in June 1968.

Germans nick-named the Frua-bodied Glas V8 coupe the
Glaserati thanks to its similarity to a certain Italian sportscar.
Pic: Nic Kische

Graber Alvis
1955–67

NUMBER BUILT: 126

Swiss coachbuilder Hermann Graber produced 126 3-litre Alvis models for wealthy Swiss clients who liked their high-quality finish and exquisite detail. Graber had an agreement with Alvis, the British manufacturer that built its cars under licence, extending the life of its chassis.

The Graber Alvis was made in a variety of two-door coupe and drophead styles that echoed the British-built version. But Graber gradually developed the shape into something more glamorous and modern, dropping the traditional Alvis grille on later 'Special' and 'Super' TD/TE/TF coupes, evolving a more slender, Italianate look and experimenting with various styles of headlights. Later cars used oblong Mercedes lights.

Alvis started making Grabers when its own car production faltered, and it had stopped by the time Graber's two-door saloon on the 3-litre Alvis was shown at the Paris show in 1955. In 1967 Alvis stopped building cars and now, sadly, the name is more synonymous with military hardware.

One owner of a Graber Alvis, who was also a Facel Vega enthusiast, loved his cars so much he changed his names to Mr Alvis Vega. Pic: John Fox

The jet set

Handsome, feted heirs to family fortunes indulged themselves on the French Riviera in the 1950s with orgies, bottles of Bollinger, bedding minor European royalty and water-skiing naked with Brigitte Bardot. They liked fast, expensive cars and regularly wrapped them around trees at high speed while over-refreshed. They wanted not just another Ferrari, but the biggest, fastest, most expensive Ferrari built to their own requirements like a suit or a pair of boots. Ferrari happily pampered the world's most decadent international playboys with its Superamerica and, later, Superfast models. Maserati countered with the 170mph 5000GT, essentially a sports racing car clothed in the most fashionable and luxurious Gran Turismo bodywork of the day (its customer base looked like a guest list for a party on a Greek shipping tycoon's luxury yacht). Connoisseurs of the ultimate exotic might have sampled a Pegaso, but few were brave enough to try.

Pegaso Z102/Z103

NUMBER BUILT: 86

Pure, uncompromising, jewel-like and hugely expensive ... that was the Pegaso GT. The car was designed to an idealised racing car specification that made other exotic cars seem ordinary, with a mere 86 built in seven years. Each was a kind of prototype, the creation of one of the 20th century's most charismatic engineers, Don Wilfrido Ricart. Formerly of Alfa Romeo, where he had famously clashed with Enzo Ferrari, Ricart joined Pegaso in 1950.

He dreamed up the Pegaso GT car project as a diversion from the daily grind of worthy truck production. The car was a government-funded public relations exercise built to show that Spain was not a rural backwater, but capable of building sophisticated, high-technology luxury goods. General Franco, Spain's leader, was among the owners.

The engine was the world's first 'production' four-camshaft V8, with twin distributors, gear drive for the cams, dry sump lubrication, fully machined internal moving parts and hugely robust bottom end. In early 2.5-litre form, the brochures talked of 140bhp with the single Weber carburettor but with more capacity (the biggest engines were 3.2 litres), higher compression, multiple carburettors and a supercharger, there was a promise of 360bhp. Even the Pegaso's most loyal followers would agree the four-cam was a flawed and over bred design, not really practical for road use. Maintenance was a nightmare: inspecting the outer camshafts meant removing the engine because they sat so tight against the walls of the bay.

Touring of Italy were the most favoured coachbuilders on the
ultra-exotic Pegaso chassis and tended to produce the most
elegant designs. Pic: Motor Trend

" Ricart dreamed up the Pegaso GT car project as a

diversion from the daily grind of worthy truck production "

Maserati 5000GT

1959-64

NUMBER BUILT: 32

The 5000GT remains the ultimate road-going Maserati, nothing less than a road-going racing car clothed in a mouth-watering selection of fashionable bodywork for an exclusive clientele. The car emerged when Maserati found it had some spare 450S sports racing cars. It was decided that, with some refinements, they could be fitted to a modified 3500GT chassis. Some customers ordered full race engines but even a standard 5000GT – retaining the gear-driven cam-drive of the 450S – produced an outrageous 170mph, with the 0-60mph dash taking 6.5 seconds. Owners included the Aga Khan (the hereditary Muslim leader) and rich industrialists looking for the ultimate in road travel. Touring of Milan did perhaps the most brutally elegant bodywork for the 5000GT while the now almost forgotten Allemano was the most prolific, clothing well over half the cars built in a coupe body that looked rather similar to the Touring design. Others, from the likes of Frua, Bertone and Pininfarina were perhaps less happy, but always glamorous.

Driving a 5000GT, you felt like king of the road. In fact you were probably a king or possibly a prince, maybe a film star or industrial tycoon. Pic: Author archive

"A road-going racing car clothed in a mouth-watering selection of fashionable bodywork for an exclusive clientele"

"Extra weight slightly blunted the performance compared to the two-wheel-drive Interceptor but the FF reached 130mph"

Jensen FF

NUMBER BUILT: 320

Of all the cars Jensen made, the FF was easily the best. The initials stood for Ferguson Formula, the four-wheel-drive system developed by Harry Ferguson that, unlike systems found on off-road vehicles, split the torque unequally between the front and rear. This gave the car unreal handling qualities for a big GT.

When combined with Dunlop Maxeret anti-lock braking (another first), it persuaded journalists to describe the FF as the world's safest car. The FF, with its distinctive Vignale shape, at first glance looked identical to the much more conventional Interceptor and indeed they had much in common. Under the bonnet was a 6.3-litre 325bhp V8, driving through a three-speed automatic transmission to a live rear axle.

The FF's wheelbase was four inches longer but the most instant recognition point was the extra vent on either front wing. Underneath, the chassis was almost totally different: the prop shaft passed along the left of the engine and gearbox and, at the front, a diff took the drive to the front wheels. Extra weight slightly blunted the performance compared to the two-wheel-drive Interceptor but the FF reached 130mph with 0-60mph taking eight seconds. Owners included Ginger Baker, the jazz, blues and R&B drummer who formed the rock band Cream in the 1960s. A series II version was introduced in 1969 with a tidied-up interior and front-end styling but sales were slow compared with the cheaper Interceptor and Jensen discontinued the FF in 1971 with 320 built.

The Jensen FF was a far better car than the Interceptor but, because it looked virtually identical, the cheaper two-wheel-drive model massively outsold it. Pic: Classic Cars

Ferrari 410
Superamerica S1, 2 & 3 1956-59

NUMBER BUILT: 38

All Ferraris were special and expensive in the 1950s but with its exclusive Superamerica series, Ferrari began to make more of a distinction between road and racing. The Superamerica was designed for a clientele who demanded the biggest engines and the most power, but were not likely to enter the car for competition. The Superamerica was about crossing continents in high-speed luxury, not winning races, and owners included Prince Bernard of Holland. The Lampredi V12 was enlarged to 5 litres and was for many years the biggest engine ever used in a road-going Ferrari. You chose your top speed according to axle ratio: 165mph was claimed for the 'long' diff but the car was so rare and exclusive this was never verified (Ferrari didn't allow journalists to road-test cars for many years to come). The 410 Superamerica is perhaps most memorable for the flamboyant designs that were perpetrated on its chassis. Perhaps the most outrageous was the Ghia Coupe with its massive tail fins inspired by the contemporary Chrysler dream cars. Pininfarina's Superfast – again with huge tail fins – was equally vulgar but great fun. The Series 3 410 Superamerica, the last Ferrari to use the Lampredi V12, had more power, bigger brakes and an improved gearbox. It tended to be clothed in fairly sober Pininfarina Coupe bodywork.

Pininfarina was becoming the dominant Ferrari chassis stylist by the time of the exclusive Superamerica series.
Pic: Pininfarina Archive.

"The Superamerica was designed for a clientele who demanded the biggest engines and the most power"

Ferrari 400
Superamerica 1959-64

NUMBER BUILT: 48

If you wanted the ultimate road-going Ferrari in the late 1950s, then you asked Mr Ferrari, very nicely, if he might like to build you a Superamerica. The 4-litre V12 engine (derived from the original 4.5-litre Grand Prix engine) was effectively an updated version of the first Ferrari engine dating back to 1946. Forty-eight of these cars were specially commissioned for an international elite that included obscure European aristocracy, playboys like Fiat boss Gianni Agnelli and tycoons such as Nelson Rockefeller.

There was no 'standard' bodywork for these luxurious, heavy Ferraris although most were completed in a variation on Pininfarina's Coupe Aerodynamico style. Agnelli's car, the first built, is probably the most memorable 400 Superamerica with its aggressive rectangular grille, panoramic windscreen and transparent roof panel. Later chassis had a slightly longer wheelbase but only the Superamerica of Mr Ferrari himself seems to have been a 2+2. If you were lucky enough to own a 400 Superamerica, then you probably had the fastest car on the public highway, capable of more than 170mph.

For most people the 400 Superfast was a mythical car only glimpsed in catalogues and car magazines. For the chosen few it was just another fast, fabulous means of transport. Pic: Pininfarina Archive

"*If you were lucky enough to own a 400 Superamerica, then you probably had the fastest car on the public highway*"

" A hefty car for special clients with the heftiest wallets, costing

twice as much as its nearest equivalent among 'ordinary' Ferraris "

The 365 California was one of the biggest Ferraris ever made and probably the last to have been personally over-seen by Battista Pininfarina. Pic: Pininfarina Archive

Ferrari 365
California Spider 1966-67

NUMBER BUILT: 14

The 365 California was the most exclusive Ferrari, with only 14 built. The first was delivered in July 1966, the last almost exactly a year later, and Ferrari must have virtually taken orders for all as soon as the model was announced.

While it shared its name with the earlier 250 California Spider, the 365 was more of a successor to the Superamerica and 500 Superfast Series: a hefty car for special clients with the heftiest wallets, costing twice as much as its nearest equivalent among 'ordinary' Ferraris, the open-topped 330GTC.

This was no taut, sinuous roadster but a full-bodied cabriolet that aimed to pamper as well as thrill. If ever a vehicle exuded the glamour of sun-baked locations and tanned 1960s playboys in millionaire beach resorts, this was it. The name, California, tells you all you need to know about the lush, easy-living market the car was designed to appeal to.

In a sense it is the last truly rare catalogued Ferrari. After the 14th and final car was built in July 1967, there would be no more special series, ultra-expensive Ferraris. There would be one-offs and show cars, and all kinds of rich men's follies, but as an exercise in flamboyant, jewel-like hand-assembled decadence, the 365 California marks the end of an era, the last of the truly coach-built Ferraris.

Facel Vega Facel II
1962-64

"The HK500 had seemed to be influenced by American

styling but the Facel II was more European "

NUMBER BUILT: 184

A ware that his HK500 was beginning to look slightly dated (the shape originated in 1954), Facel Vega boss Jean Daninos had a new body created for the car in 1962. Lower and more angular, in the early 1960s idiom, the Facel II had Mercedes-style headlamps flanking a smaller version of the Facel grille. The HK500 had seemed to be influenced by American styling but the Facel II was more European, with generally less glitz.

Mechanically, the car was much as before and was offered with the same choice of twin- or single-carburettor Chrysler engines linked either to four-speed manual transmission or a three-speed Chrysler automatic. Unlike the HK500, which used TV-style push button selection for the automatic transmission, the Facel II had a conventional floor shift. Dunlop disc brakes were used all round and power steering, leather seats and electric windows were all standard on this expensive car. Owners included actor Tony Curtis and Beatles drummer Ringo Starr, and others who could afford a car costing the equivalent of two Jaguar E-types and a Lotus Elan on the British market.

The Facel II was the last and best of the big two-door V8 Facel
Vegas and the most glamorous of the Euro-American GT cars.
Pic: Richard Stevens

Britt Ekland was quite an enthusiast of the V8 Bristol and shared many passions with Peter Sellers, including a love of cars. Pic: Author Archive

Bristol 407
Viotti Convertible 1962-64

NUMBER BUILT: 1

Actor Peter Sellers – a habitual car buyer – was a friend of Tony Crook, motor dealer and managing director of Britain's Bristol Cars. Sellers was ripped off by the motor trade so often that he enlisted Crook to buy and sell cars for him. On a visit to Bristol's showroom in London, Sellers spotted a one-off Viotti convertible that had recently been completed on a 407 saloon chassis (the first of the V8 Bristols) and bought it on the spot. It was used by his then wife, the actress Britt Ekland.

Elegant in profile, but rather bland at the front, the Viotti was a practical four-seater open car with an easily raised and lowered hood. Sellers and Ekland didn't keep the car for long – the actor changed cars almost as often as most people change socks – but it was used for many years by Tony Crook's daughter, Carol. It is now owned by a Bristol enthusiast in Scotland.

The other one-off special body on the 407 chassis was by Zagato. 'It was front-heavy but it went like a rocket,' recalled Tony Crook. 'We had it as a demo car and my daughter Carol drove it. So did Britt Ekland: they used to compare notes about driving it from Surrey to central London in the middle of the night.'

" Sellers and Ekland didn't keep the car for long – the actor changed cars almost as often as most people change socks "

Ferrari 500 Superfast

1964–66

NUMBER BUILT: 37

There's a tendency to think of all Ferraris as low-slung and noisy, but Enzo Ferrari knew he had an international clientele wanting something different. There were ultra-rich customers willing to pay extra for a big, comfortable, very fast and rare Ferrari. The 500 Superfast was the flagship Ferrari touring car because of its high performance, high price and rarity (37 were built, hand-crafted by Pininfarina at the rate of one or two a month). The 500 Superfast continued Enzo's Aerodynamico Coupe theme from the Super America series. Its engine was a V12, of course, but unique to the Superfast, a 'long block' 5-litre unit rated at 400bhp that would take the car to more than 170mph. Owners included the actor Peter Sellers and the Shah of Iran, a hugely wealthy collector of the finest cars.

The last 12 Superfast are unofficial series II models with a five-speed gearbox replacing the overdrive, vented front wings and top-hinged pedals. Seven Superfasts were bought in the UK and the last was bought by the country's Ferrari concessionaire, Col Ronnie Hoare. The 1965 London Motor Show car was written off by its second owner who died in the crash.

The 170mph 500 Superfast was one of the world's most expensive cars, especially when hand-finished in the Pininfarina factory. Pic: Pininfarina Archive

"There were ultra-rich customers willing to pay extra

for a big, comfortable, very fast and rare Ferrari"

Rare supercars

We tend to associate the supercar, at its worst, with the excesses of the 1980s: massively wide mid-engined cars with skirts and spoilers driven by ageing heart-throbs with bleached mullet hairdos. Very *Miami Vice*. There are no Miami Vice cars here, but America's supercharged Cord was a supercar of its day – and rare – but you'd look daft driving one in a white Armani suit (it was more a cravat and sports jacket car). The Bizzarrini, Aston DB4 GT and Jaguar XKSS were really competition cars with a thin veneer of road-going civility but would have been mind-blowing to drive on the public highway 30 or 40 years ago. The Mercedes C111 earns its place because it is one of the finest things I've ever driven. And then there's the Monteverdi Hai ... it proves generations of civilisation and neutrality in Switzerland have given us more than the cuckoo clock.

Fiat 8V

NUMBER BUILT: 114

Fiat first mooted a flagship V8 model in the late 1940s but the big saloon prototype proved too heavy and slothful. Fiat's top management was not impressed and the project lost momentum. That left a 70-degree, 2-litre V8 engine going begging: so why not fit it to a sports car? Enter the Otto Vu, launched at the Geneva motor show in 1952. One of the fastest 2-litre cars of the 1950s, the 8V is the only production V8-engined car ever made by Fiat.

The shape may have been an in-house Fiat effort but it vied with the best work from Italian coachbuilders for elegant purity. The 8V was as slippery as it looked and chief Fiat test driver Carlo Salomano recorded a two-way maximum of 207kph (129mph) on the Turin-Milan autostrada.

Fiat design boss Dante Giacosa raided the parts bins to produce an exceptionally accomplished chassis, using Fiat 1100 independent suspension front and rear. Bodies for the 8V were built at Lingotto by Fiat in its experimental coachwork department, with local specialist Siata contracted to produce the mechanical elements. Fiat built 114 Otto Vu chassis but not all had the standard Fiat body. Vignale, Bertone, Ghia and Pininfarina all clothed the 8V, and Fiat built a special plastic-bodied version of the standard car as a motor show one-off.

Unknown rally entrants in a Fiat 8V: this 2-litre Coupe is Fiat's only V8-engined car. Pic: Author archive

"*One of the fastest 2-litre cars of the 1950s, the 8V is*

the only production V8-engined car ever made by Fiat"

Cord 812 Supercharged

NUMBER BUILT: 64

Styling alone gains the Cord 812 instant entry to any shortlist of ultimate 1930s cars of any nationality. It was an assertive essay in futuristic elegance that is distinctively American.

The outer visuals were true to the sophisticated mechanisms that lay beneath the skin. Front-wheel drive (like Citroens, Cords had gearboxes and differentials mounted off the front of the engine) and independent front suspension in a low-slung unitary shell gave it an assured touch through curves. The 170bhp from a whispering supercharged V8 engine ensured a 100mph-plus stride.

In supercharged form, it had stainless steel exhaust headers exiting from either side of the bonnet and was, in today's terms, a genuine supercar that quickly captured the attention of the wealthy. They fell in love with the image it projected of cutting-edge glamour, the perfect complement to a house designed by Frank Lloyd Wright (for many, America's greatest 20th century architect). Orders flooded in after the car's debut at the 1936 New York Auto Show. Buyers promised early delivery were fobbed off with a scale model as Cord's engineers struggled with the intricacies of the gearbox. The first Cord 810s suffered from a series of mechanical problems. Out of 2,992 810/812 series cars, only 688 were supercharged, with only 64 of those having the most desirable Sportsman open body.

In the aristocracy of pre-war American classics, the supercharged Cord convertible is about as blue-blooded as it gets.

With its pop-up lights and coffin-nosed bonnet, the Cord was highly futuristic but technical problems scuppered the car early in its career. Pic: Giles Chapman Archive

"In the aristocracy of pre-war American classics, the supercharged

Cord convertible is about as blue-blooded as it gets"

Sportsman

BMW M1

NUMBER BUILT: 456

To replace its CSL coupe in group five racing, BMW needed a mid-engined chassis worthy of its twin-cam 3.5-litre straight-six. Four hundred of the cars would have to be built over two years to qualify for the formula.

BMW Motorsport hired Lamborghini to develop the mid-engined M1 coupe. In turbo group five form, it gave up to 700bhp but for the road, BMW deemed 277bhp enough. Lamborghini was to build prototypes and assemble the 400 road cars required for homologation at the rate of two a week.

Prototypes were tested in 1977 but Lamborghini was in deep financial trouble and BMW transferred final production to Baur in Stuttgart. The car was launched in late1978, coinciding with new group five regulations saying 400 road cars had to be sold before a version could be raced.

The M1 was entered in the Procar series that pitched top-level Grand Prix drivers against each other in identical 470bhp group four M1 racers. For two seasons (1979-80) it was a crowd-pleaser, with Niki Lauda (who bought a road version), Nelson Piquet and other F1 stars heading the grid in factory-backed M1s against eager owner-drivers. The M1 racer was never much more than a promising also-ran but the road car was one of the best. For the price of two top-flight BMW 6-Series coupes, you got a supercar that wasn't just fast (M1s were independently clocked at 161mph) but comfortable, refined, surprisingly frugal and beautifully built.

The M1 was an effective flagship for BMW, a disaster in its intended role as a competition car but a remarkably civilised supercar. Pic: Author archive

" *The M1 racer was never much more than a promising*

also-ran but the road car was one of the best "

"As a long-distance sports racing car, it had pace and stamina

and Bizzarrini regarded it as a better car than his GTO"

The Bizzarrini came too late to compete with the new
generation of mid-engined sports racing cars but made a
thrilling road car for the few who could run to it.
Pic: Jason Yorke Edgill

Bizzarrini GT Strada

NUMBER BUILT: ABOUT 133

Intellectually, if not literally, the Bizzarrini GT Strada was the successor to the 250GTO its designer, Giotto Bizzarrini, had engineered for Ferrari. As a long-distance sports racing car, it had pace and stamina and Bizzarrini regarded it as a better car than his GTO which was overshadowed by a new generation of mid-engined cars like the Ferrari 250LM and Ford GT40.

Giotto Bizzarrini wanted to go racing to give the fledgling Iso marque (for which he was then designing a new GT car) some credibility. Iso boss Renzo Rivolta was unconvinced, but happy to allow his engineering consultant to design a racer based on the new Grifo. Thus, the car was launched at the 1963 Turin motor show as a much lighter competition version of the new Iso Grifo, called A3/C (C stood for competizione). At some point in 1965, Bizzarrini fell out with Rivolta, perhaps because Giotto was calling his cars Bizzarrini Grifos rather than Iso Grifos. Rivolta cut off Bizzarrini's supply of parts but failed to take account of his rival's crafty nature. He'd sneakily registered the Grifo name on his own. Suddenly Rivolta realised he could not call his car a Grifo unless Bizzarrini agreed. Thus, a deal was struck whereby Giotto got the bits to build 50 cars while handing the Grifo name back to Iso. Around 133 GT Stradas were built before Bizzarrini succumbed to financial problems in 1968.

Aston Martin
V8 Zagato 1986-89

NUMBER BUILT: 50

The 186mph Aston Martin V8 Zagato remains one of the most collectable post-war Aston Martins. It was the first two-seater Aston since the DB4 GT, production was limited to 50 and its phenomenal speed was headline news in Britain. It was priced at $102,000/£70,000 but the whole production run was sold before a single car was built. With exclusivity assured, greedy investors bought Zagatos and sold them at anything up to $730,000/£500,000 on the open market. The Zagato had a far more slippery profile than the standard Aston Vantage, was 10 per cent lighter and carried a more powerful (432bhp) version of the quad-camshaft, 5.3-litre Vantage engine. A French magazine recorded its 0-60mph time as 4.8 seconds.

Not everyone liked Zagato's shape. The double-bubble roof seemed superfluous and the grille unresolved. In profile the awkwardly angled C-pillar dropped away to a truncated tail, where most of the length (the Zagato was 16 inches shorter than the standard V8) was amputated.

Two a month were built between 1986 and 1988 if you don't count the prototype and a run of 25 truly hideous convertibles. Orders worth $10.2m/£7m were placed on the strength of a styling sketch and once values started to rocket, Aston raised the retail price to reflect the then crazy open market. Owners included actor Rowan Atkinson, of Mr Bean movie fame. When the investor market peaked in the late 1980s, many speculators lost heavily as the values of these cars halved almost overnight.

Not one of Zagato's proudest moments – its interpretation of the V8 looked particularly bizzare in convertible form. Pic: Aston Martin Lagonda

Aston Martin
DB4 GT Zagato 1961-63

NUMBER BUILT: 19

The DB4 GT Zagato is the most sought-after post-war Aston Martin because only 19 were built. It was designed to take on the Ferrari 250 SWB in GT racing but the competition career of the Zagato, though glorified by such star name drivers as Moss, Salvadori and Clark, was brief and only fairly distinguished. As a road car it left something to be desired compared with the relatively refined 'standard' DB4 GT, even for the well-heeled sporting gents who fancied themselves as weekend racers. They were lighter than the standard item but the build quality was sketchy, historically par for the course with Zagato bodywork.

Production was erratic and long-winded: the chassis were sent from Britain to Italy to be bodied, and then returned to the UK for trim. Aston had trouble selling them, which is hard to believe in view of the high prices they now raise at auction.

At 314bhp the Zagato was 12 horsepower stronger than the standard twin-plug GT engine, enough to give a top speed of 153mph and acceleration that set new standards of ferocity for a road car. Aston guaranteed 0-100mph in 14 seconds.

The muscular DB4 GT Zagato makes collectors go weak at the knees and is possibly the ultimate Aston Martin.
Pic: Aston Martin Lagonda

" *The competition career of the Zagato, though glorified by such star name drivers as Moss, Salvadori and Clark, was brief and only fairly distinguished* "

Toyota 2000GT 1967-70

NUMBER BUILT: 337

The Toyota 2000GT was, surely, the ultimate Japanese classic that mixed the best European practice of the day in a curvy, aggressive coupe of rare elegance. The 2000GT was an aborted Nissan sports car project taken on by Toyota as an image-boosting exercise. Its straight-six twin-cam engine was based on the iron block of the Toyota Crown and developed 150bhp (racing versions could be tuned to give more than 200). The 2000GT, with Lotus-style chassis and coil spring/A-arm suspension, would do nearly 140mph. The car had a super-slick five-speed transmission and handled like the thoroughbred it undoubtedly was, with sharp steering and a surprisingly supple ride. It was a serious portent of just what the Japanese were capable of, at a time when Europeans still regarded their products as marginal. Despite rave reviews in the specialist press, and the appearance of the convertible version in the James Bond film *You only live twice*, only 11 Americans ever bought 2000GTs. The truth was it was too expensive and buyers turned their noses up at the cheaper single-cam version that accounted for nine of the 337 2000GTs built. Of the three shipped to Britain, two were used on the Bond film, and the third was sold to Twiggy, the Swinging Sixties superstar model. Today, collectors jostle to buy a 2000GT when one comes up for sale, particularly the Japanese, who recognise the car as their only credible big sports car of the 1960s.

Made famous by its role in the James Bond film You Only Live Twice, the Toyota 2000GT was the first Japanese car to be taken seriously by collectors due to its driver appeal, looks and rarity. Pic: Author archive

"It was a serious portent of just what the Japanese were capable of"

" The few who did try the car reported unruly handling, particularly in the wet "

Monteverdi Hai

NUMBER BUILT: 2

The Monteverdi Hai is a kind of mythical supercar, because few journalists were allowed to test it, and virtually no one else has seen one. Peter Monteverdi had been building Chrysler-engined GT cars in Switzerland since 1967, and they were handsome coupes cast in the mould of England's Jensen and Bristol models. The Hai of 1970 was Monteverdi's bid for the mid-engined supercar market whose only player at that point was the Lamborghini Miura.

The Hai was a far cruder machine, with its Chrysler 'Hemi' engine protruding into the passenger compartment, and De Dion rear suspension based on the type found on his 375 series front-engined cars. Space was tight in the Hai, which had no room for a spare wheel, and very little for luggage. It was well equipped though, and even had air conditioning as standard. The styling had a certain brutal charm and was the work of Monteverdi himself with help from Fissore, which also built the light-alloy body shell.

Top speed was said to be 169mph, but this was never verified, and the few who did try the car reported unruly handling, particularly in the wet. The Hai remained on Monteverdi price lists until 1977 but only two were sold.

The Monteverdi Hai had a claimed top speed of 169mph, a tendency to take off at high speed and was generally difficult to drive. Pic: Jason Yorke Edgill

Lancia Hyena

1992-94

NUMBER BUILT: 24

The inspiration for the Lancia Hyena came from Paul Koot, a Dutch private car dealer and collector. Visiting the Zagato factory in 1990, he bemoaned the fact that there were no more specialist coach-built versions of Lancia production cars. Virtually on the spot, Andrea Zagato produced a picture of his vision of a coupe based on the Lancia Integrale, and before long there were plans to enter production. The Integrale EVO was used as a basis but the Hyena was much more than a rebodied Lancia saloon. Zagato built a steel frame on the Integrale's four-wheel-drive floorpan, and fashioned a hunched, muscular coupe body around it using aluminium and Kevlar. Koot gained permission from Lancia to use the corporate front grille but by the time the car was ready to go into production, Fiat-Lancia proved distinctly unhelpful in supplying components to build the cars. Zagato had to cut up virtually complete cars which sent the price of the Hyena through the roof. Unsurprisingly, the project soon died, which was a great shame, as the Hyena was a fabulous car – lighter, faster and even more agile than the rally-winning Integrale.

Foolishly, Fiat/Lancia didn't give its blessing to this privately backed venture, jealous perhaps that they hadn't thought of it themselves. Pic: Giles Chapman Archive

"The project soon died, which was a great shame, as the Hyena was a fabulous car"

Jaguar XKSS

NUMBER BUILT: 16

The XKSS was devised by Jaguar when 25 of the original batch of 67 production D-Types remained unsold after the factory's temporary retirement from racing in 1956. The sub-plot motivation was to make the D-Type acceptable to the Sports Car Club of America as a road machine: the SCCA decreed that 50 of these revised road-going models had to be built if the sports racing Jaguar was to be eligible.

Thus, by removing head fairing and the central division between the driver and passenger, adding an extra door, a full-width framed windscreen and rudimentary hood with side screen and an exhaust cowling, D-Type became the XKSS.

The aluminium body was protected at each corner by slim bumpers cut down from saloon car pressings. Like the D-Type that spawned it, the 150mph, 250bhp XKSS was so flexible and tractable you could use it to go shopping and on its tall 16in Dunlop tyres, it had all the poise and balance of its race car sibling. The result was enough to attract film icon Steve McQueen, a fast-car enthusiast.

Jaguar planned an initial run of 21 but only 16 had been built when the remaining five D-Type shells (along with the tooling) perished in a factory fire in February 1957. Of the 16 XKSS (all right-hand drive), 12 went to the USA, two to Canada and one to Hong Kong. Only one stayed in Britain, though a couple of D-Types were converted retrospectively to XKSS specification.

The most famous XKSS owner was legendary movie star Steve McQueen who terrorised his local neighbourhood in the 170mph two-seater. Pic: Pictorial Press

" *The 150mph, 250bhp XKSS was so flexible*

and tractable you could use it to go shopping "

"*In the right hands these elegant, well-engineered*

cars were as quick as anything on the road"

Iso Grifo 7-litre
1962-1974

NUMBER BUILT: 90

Iso of Italy started manufacturing in the mid-1950s, producing Isetta bubble cars (also built under licence by BMW), but in 1962 it decided to enter the high-class GT car market with the Rivolta. A Bertone-styled, four-seater coupe with a box-section frame, and DeDion rear suspension, it was powered by a Corvette V8 engine, so performance was abundant (up to 140mph) and fully exploited through the manual gearbox. The Rivolta was well received but it was not until the debut of the Grifo a year later that the fledgling supercar builder really made its mark.

By shortening the Rivolta, and clothing it in a sensational coupe body (again by Bertone), Iso had a car to challenge Ferrari. The original 5.4-litre V8 was tuned to 300 and 365bhp, with a top speed of up to 160mph in its most potent form. The ultimate version was the 390bhp 7-litre, built from 1968 to challenge the Ferrari Daytona and Maserati Ghibli. Iso claimed 170mph for this flagship coupe.

Naturally, four-wheel disc brakes were deemed necessary for a car of such weight and power and in the right hands these elegant, well-engineered cars were as quick as anything on the road. For the last two years of production, Iso used Ford 'Cleveland' V8s rather than Corvette engines. By then Iso was on the rocks financially and died in the midst of the 1974 fuel crisis.

Fully sorted, the C111 prototype could have developed into a great flagship supercar for Mercedes.
Pic: DaimlerChrysler Archive

Mercedes
C111 Rotary 1970

NUMBER BUILT: 3

The Mercedes C111 was the fabulous mid-engined supercar that never went on sale, to the great frustration of the famous and wealthy itching to add one to their collections. Mercedes own the only three built before the company decided not to go ahead with a full production run. The C111 Rotary would have turned the supercar establishment on its head, for it was undoubtedly superior to anything being produced by Ferrari and Lamborghini at the time. The cars were startlingly brutal rather than beautiful: painted orange, they looked like giant versions of toy maker Corgi's Whizzwheels. The C111 had trademark gullwing doors that brought Mercedes' last supercar to mind, the 300SL. The first two were powered by a dual rotor Wankel engine equivalent to 3,600cc that produced 300bhp and 170mph. The engine was tucked down in a small space between the rear seats, driving through a five-speed ZF transaxle and flanked by the deep sills of the platform chassis, which doubled as fuel tanks. A third car had a quad rotor engine – equivalent to 4800c – which could swish the C111 to an effortless 187mph. They were fabulous to drive and, unlike most Italian supercars, as professionally finished as production vehicles. A fourth C111 was built for record breaking in 1976, and another in 1978, but these differed from the original trio. Mercedes had seen the future and it wasn't a Wankel: the final C111s were diesel-powered.

"They were fabulous to drive and, unlike most Italian supercars,

as professionally finished as production vehicles "

The 200mph club

Ferrari, Bugatti, Mercedes, Porsche and McLaren ... these are the breeds in this ultra-exclusive 200mph club that maybe represents the Indian summer of the supercar, as speed becomes an anti-social activity akin to smoking in the US and Europe. Once, a reliable, practical 200mph road car was highly improbable. Engines were powerful enough but tyre technology and the science of aerodynamics surely could not allow us to enjoy that kind of speed in safety, even where legal. Now, the introduction of yet another 200mph car seems almost routine, though they are vastly expensive and usually totally impractical. Tax-exile rock stars, sporting superstars and randomly wealthy individuals having a mid-life crisis (who will never get the cars out of third gear in case they ruffle their hair-dos) queue up to be the first to own these status symbols. In some cases, the cars are so exclusive you have to be invited by the maker to buy one; no riff-raff you see ...

Mercedes-Benz CLK GTR

2001

NUMBER BUILT: 25

At $1.57m/£1.1m, the Mercedes CLK GTR is the most expensive road car ever put on the market and was the road-going version of the car that competed in the Le Mans 24-Hour race. Built by AMG, its bizarre carbon fibre shell hid a 604bhp, V12 engine limited to 199mph. The 25 cars built in accordance with the homologation safety rules (so the car could be sold to be used on public roads) took nearly three years to put together and were genuinely road-friendly with comforts like air conditioning and an acoustic parking aid.

But you would only take it to go shopping once: the hair-trigger throttle and a needlessly awkward gearbox might just be a liability when parking in a tight space.

They might even be a problem on the road because the combination of a paddle shift and a clutch pedal (that has to be slammed hard before you can get a gear) doesn't make for seamless deployment of the CLK's massive urge. The performance is awesome: 0-60mph in 3.8 seconds, 0-125mph in 9.9 seconds), and grip is engineered to match the speed. The CLK GTR is a fabulous hunk of technology that should be a must for any serious collector of ultimate Mercs.

Stripped of the stickers, this was more or less what Mercedes sold to the public but the CLK required expert drivers. Pic: DaimlerChrsyler Archive

" *The CLK GTR is a fabulous hunk of technology that should*

be a must for any serious collector of ultimate Mercs "

McLaren F1 1993-97

NUMBER BUILT: 100

As a high-performance road car, there is still little to challenge the McLaren F1. Designer Gordon Murray, the man behind McLaren's F1 cars, had a long-held ambition to build a road car, the fastest and most exciting yet that was also docile enough to drive in town. His vision called for a dramatic mid-engined three-seater, with the driver sitting in the middle, and a very low weight of 1,000kg. Lotus Elan stylist Peter Stevens was commissioned to pen the car's shape, while BMW Motorsport agreed to design an all-new 627bhp, 6064cc four-cam V12 engine.

The result was a 231mph projectile capable of 0-60mph in 3.2 sec, 0-100mph in 6.3 sec. Priced $950,000/£635,000, it was a hugely labour intensive car to produce and featured many space-age materials in its construction, not to mention gold leaf. Despite its price, the McLaren was probably uneconomical to make.

The F1 was almost invincible on the track: the F1 GTR won all but two of its GT endurance races, while the F1 was triumphant at Le Mans in 1995. Only 100 F1s were built, a third of the original projection, because many who put their names down for the car melted away. Celebrity buyers included former Beatle George Harrison but production ended in late 1997.

For many who count themselves as high-class drivers, the F1
remains the greatest of them all: uncompromising, expensive
and ultra quick. Pic Gus Gregory

Ferrari F40

NUMBER BUILT: 1,200

The F40, built to mark Enzo Ferrari's 40th year as a car maker in 1988, was also intended to represent the supercar in its ultimate form. Outwardly, the shape owed something to the contemporary 328GTB, but the car was much wider and more aggressive, with a rear hoop spoiler and an uncompromisingly chopped tail. Based on the floorpan of the 288GTO and retaining the classic tubular steel frame, it made extensive use of weight-saving composite materials.

The latest Formula One turbo technology was applied to a special, short-stroke 3-litre V8, and twin turbos were used for an output of 478bhp (Ferrari claimed a top speed of 201mph). The F40 was sensationally fast and incredibly noisy, with the cabin (bereft of carpets) acting like a sound box. The stripped-out and rather austere interior further reinforced the impression that the F40 was a racing car for the road, although ironically the cars were never raced in anger. Many were bought as investments and such was the demand that Ferrari more than doubled the original intended production run to 1,200.

It was raw and aggressive but, in supercar terms, the F40 isn't that rare as 1,200 were built. Pic: Author archive

"The F40 was sensationally fast and incredibly noisy,

with the cabin (bereft of carpets) acting like a sound box"

"With the engine rigidly mounted to the chassis,

the noise was incredible, both in volume and quality"

Ferrari F50

NUMBER BUILT: 349

When the time came to build a new flagship, the brief for Ferrari's engineers was simple and uncompromising: take our 1990 Formula One racer (the 641/2), and transform it into a street-legal 200mph road car.

Enter, in March 1995, the F50, a two-seat V12 carbon fibre, 200mph mid-engined sports car. Clothed in a Pininfarina body that recalled Ferrari's sports racers of the early 1970s, the F50 was easily the wildest road-going car ever built by Ferrari, though that claim to fame was later taken by the Enzo.

Ferrari decreed that only 349 F50s would be built, compared with 1,311 F40s, Ferrari's previous 'ultimate' road car. With 520bhp coming from the F1-derived V12, the F50 would hurry to 64mph in first, 112mph in second, 138mph in fourth, 160mph in fifth and 202mph in sixth. The handling was much more forgiving than the F40 despite the extra speed, but with the engine rigidly mounted to the chassis, the noise was incredible, both in volume and quality.

The F50 took the cult of the hypercar to new and more ludicrous heights with its extreme width, outrageous noise and extreme speed. Pic: Lynx Motors International

Bugatti EB110

NUMBER BUILT: AROUND 135

The last true Bugattis were built in the early 1950s but the brand was revived in 1991 by Italian car dealer Romano Artioli, who somehow found the backing to produce a lavish mid-engined supercar. It had all the right ingredients for success. The body was styled by Marcello Gandini and the new factory was built in the Modena region of Italy where Artioli – who later bought Lotus from GM – could recruit people brought up building Lamborghinis, Maseratis and locally made Ferraris. Engineers were also head-hunted from Audi and Lotus. Powered by a 3.5-litre V12 with four turbos and making 553bhp, the car lived up to its promise as a thrill machine with a 209mph top speed and a 3.6-second 0-60 time.

Some reckoned the four-wheel-drive chassis lacked ultimate agility and sparkle, and not everyone liked the styling. While the interior made headlines with its fitted luggage, the dashboard could have been lifted from a suburban luxobarge, and just didn't look special enough for a $490,000/£285,000 supercar. The EB110 had promise but Artioli's timing was out: a recession in the early 1990s, combined with the Bugatti name meaning little to most supercar buyers, conspired to close down the lavish factory. Volkswagen Group paid Artioli $34m/£20m for the rights to the Bugatti name but are yet to do anything significant with it.

The EB110 seemed to be the long-awaited credible attempt to revive the Bugatti name but the project floundered in a financial crisis and the brand is now owned by Volkswagen Group. Pic: Giles Chapman Archive

"Some reckoned the four-wheel-drive chassis lacked ultimate agility and sparkle, and not everyone liked the styling"

"Drive the CL65 and you are pulling velocities

that could get you locked up in no time at all "

AMG CL65

NUMBER BUILT: STILL IN PRODUCTION

We associate 612bhp with drag racers or hyper-cars like the McLaren F1, but since the end of 2003 you have been able to access that kind of urge within the sober environment of a Mercedes CL Coupe or S-Class sedan.

By uprating the Mercedes V12 engine to a 6-litre and plumbing in a new bi-turbo system, Stuttgart's long-time power specialist AMG created the most powerful road car ever sold by the manufacturer. It is probably the most potent series production engine on the planet.

The big AMG Mercedes does not look like a hotrod, and big spoilers, vulgar wheels and gull-wing doors are notably absent. Only subtle side-skirts and AMG badging lets lesser beings know you are driving perhaps the ultimate Mercedes this side of an SLR.

A single engineer hand-assembles each AMG bi-turbo engine ('signing' it on completion) and owners want for nothing in terms of luxurious fittings that include an electrically operated rear window blind. Drive the CL65 and you are pulling velocities that could get you locked up in no time at all. In derestricted form it will easily beat 200mph, with 0-60mph taking 4.4 seconds.

Active suspension does a fine job in minimising roll, squat and dive but some motoring journalists feel the CL65 fails to match the excellence of the Bentley Continental GT. Nit-picking stuff but in the rarified world of ultimate GTs, the nits are there to be picked.

The svelte coupe shape wouldn't attract stares at an owner's golf club but it hides a 612bhp engine delivering more torque than any other current production unit. Pic: DaimlerChrysler

Ferrari Enzo

NUMBER BUILT: MAXIMUM OF 399

Ferraris are by no means as rare and exclusive as they used to be. Once they were the preserve of tycoons, rock gods and film stars; now you're quite likely to see a minor sports player behind the wheel of a second-hand 355. To maintain Ferrari's status, company boss Luca di Montezemolo recognised it needed a limited edition model cast in the mould of its 288GTO, F40 and F50, a focused ultra high-performance car fusing F1 technology with the requirements of road-going use. A car so fast, expensive and exclusive you had to be invited by the factory to buy one. Enter, in 2002, the 660bhp Enzo, which is beautiful or brutally ugly depending on your point of view. Its handling was honed by Ferrari Grand Prix hero Michael Schumacher and is the nearest mere mortals will get to experiencing Formula 1 car dynamics, with its power, paddle-shift gears and a fabulous wall of noise from behind. With a top speed of 218mph and 0-60mph in 3.65 seconds the Enzo is still not as quick as the McLaren F1 but its performance is easy to access and reassurance comes from fabulous brakes. So even minor driving talents should feel flattered behind the wheel.

It's named after the founder, and Ferrari will only sell you an
Enzo if they like you ... but the car is sold out anyway.
Pic: Gus Gregory

" *A car so fast, expensive and exclusive you*

had to be invited by the factory to buy one "

" The oddball styling strikes a bum note but those who

experience the car seem able to forgive it anything "

Pagani Zonda C12S

NUMBER BUILT: 35 UP TO SEPTEMBER 2003

The Zonda was the dream project of Horacio Pagani, a schoolboy car enthusiast who at 26 left his native Argentina for Italy and a job in Lamborghini's bodyshop. He worked his way up the hierarchy to become a stylist and, after penning the face-lifted LM002 in the mid 1990s, set up on his own with a mission to build the ultimate road going supercar. With the help of fellow countryman Juan Manuel Fangio, president of Mercedes-Benz Argentina, Pagani was able to source his engines from AMG, the Mercedes tuning specialist.

The car was to be called the Fangio F1 but when the former world champion died 1995, Pagani changed the name to Zonda, a wind that blows through the Andes. To earn credibility, the Zonda had to be better than the opposition and in many ways it does move the hyper car game forward with a magnificent chassis, great build quality and an unexpectedly high-class interior. Such cars normally suffer from wonky stitching, dodgy Fiat Uno switches and brittle trim but the futuristic Zonda sets new standards. The oddball styling strikes a bum note but those who experience the car seem able to forgive it anything.

With a top speed of 220mph and 0-60mph in a perception-warping 3.3 seconds, the 7.3-litre V12 Zonda stunned the critics who, following the demise of the Cizeta V16T and Bugatti projects had grown wary of short-lived upstart challengers to the established supercar clan. The Zonda should have a long-term future.

The Zonda is fit to challenge the greatest names in
supercar-dom and might well go the distance.
Pic: Gus Gregory

Utility cars
of the super rich

Shooting brakes, estates and station wagons based on upmarket cars seem to have been a curiously British endeavour, though American woodies of the 1930s, 40s and 50s were at times inspired. These luxurious cars have a curiously enigmatic quality over and above the vehicle they are based on, and it is not always merely a question of rarity value. Very upmarket utility cars either totally enhance the model that they are based on or appear to come from the AMC Pacer/British Austin Allegro school of automotive design. The Fiat 130 Maremma, Jaguar County Mk II and Vanden Plas 3-litre Princess Countryman fall into the first category while the Jaguar XJ6 Avon Stevens Estate goes into the second. This is the key question: would I want to be seen grouse-shooting or cruising the desert in one of these cars? The answer to all is probably 'yes'.

Who needs a Hummer when you've got one of these, a militarised 125mph V12 monster built specifically for the middle eastern market. Pic: Author archive

" *Lamborghini claimed 125mph flat out ... and single figure fuel consumption, which explained the 62-gallon fuel tank* "

Lamborghini LM 002

NUMBER BUILT: 140

The LM 002 began life as the rear-V8-engined Cheetah in the late 1970s and was essentially a massive tubular frame, clad in an uncompromisingly square plastic body with four aluminium doors. It set itself apart from lesser off-roaders in its use of all independent suspension and a protected underside that didn't leave the exhaust or gearbox vulnerable even on the most unforgiving terrain. Lamborghini V12 production cars of the 1980s had the engine at the front, delivering 450bhp through a five-speed gearbox hitched to a two-speed transfer 'splitter' giving 10 ratios to play with. Part-time four-wheel drive with freewheeling front hubs could be locked in manually for off-road use. Lamborghini claimed 125mph flat out, 0-60mph in 8.5 seconds and single figure fuel consumption, which explained the 62-gallon fuel tank.

Most of the 140 made (production finished in 1992) were sold to Middle Eastern armed forces or, in a more luxurious form, to private owners including the Sultan of Brunei. When the military found their LMs too complex to service they were passed on to civilians and they found favour as hunting vehicles.

Radford Bentley
Mk VI Countryman 1951–59

NUMBER BUILT: 6

Coachbuilder to the stars Harold Radford (he of the luxurious Radford Mini, much favoured by London's most fashionable in-crowd) built a handful of specially equipped Bentleys for Britain's wealthiest horsey set. The most famous was the Mk VI Countryman which, in addition to the normal Bentley refinements, had flasks and tumblers in the armrests, Asprey glasses and room for a hamper in the rear load area which was accessed through a split tailgate. The rear seats folded to take fishing rods and any other equipment associated with upmarket country pursuits. Countryman options were offered on the S Series cars also. Again, decanters, tumblers and flasks were hidden in doors and armrests to allow the owner and his friends to indulge in a few drinks before, after or during a day's racing. Open the boot, and you'd find a kettle and washbasin. Perhaps the ultimate was Radford's Rolls-Royce Safari car, a shooting brake conversion of a Silver Cloud Saloon. Just two were built.

Outwardly the Bentley Countryman had only gentle
modifications but internally featured every comfort
for the well-heeled sporting gent.
Pic: Frank Dale & Stepsons

"*The rear seats folded to take fishing rods and any other*

equipment associated with upmarket country pursuits"

Vanden Plas estates
1963-66

NUMBER BUILT: 7

When you've got a large estate, then a large estate car is always useful, which is why the Queen ordered a Countryman conversion on a Vanden Plas 3-litre saloon in 1963. In the early 1960s, BMC (now MG Rover) was keen to sell an upmarket estate to the Queen, who was seen in a Vauxhall Cresta Friary estate (a car more associated with Teddy boys than monarchs). The Queen specified various extras including a special roof-rack for taking fishing rods. It took a year to build, and a further six were built for exclusive customers.

With its split tailgate, folding seats and big load area, the VP Countryman was perfect for the Queen to take a trip down to the stables at Balmoral, which was where this car, finished in bottle green, saw the most use. The Queen put in another order in 1966 for a 4-litre R version but, rumour has it, this was written off by one of the Royals at Balmoral and now languishes in a secret location. But does the 3-litre still exist? We'd love to know ...

Ideal for country pursuits the Vanden Plas Countryman was exclusive to special customers. This Radford variant was commissioned by the Dupont family.
Pic: Giles Chapman Archive

"The VP Countryman was perfect for the Queen

to take a trip down to the stables at Balmoral"

Lynx Eventer

1982-2001

NUMBER BUILT: APPROX 65

The job of building the 'ultimate' shooting break as a worthy successor to the Aston Martin eventually fell to Jaguar specialist Lynx which, in 1982, came up with the XJ-S Eventer.

The ugly buttresses of the factory coupe were swapped at last for a long, graceful roof and an exquisitely shaped tapering rear side window styled by Chris Keith Lucas of Lynx. Pininfarina could not have done it better and the impractical XJ-S 2+2 was transformed into a useful four-seater, with the bonus of much better over-the-shoulder vision. It was such an obvious conversion: it makes you wonder why Jaguar did not do it.

Lynx fitted a pressed-out, ripple-free one-piece roof and the rear bulkhead was moved back, adding 3.5 inches of legroom in the rear. On early cars, the tailgate was adapted from the one fitted to the Citroen Ami estate, which must be rarer in the UK now than an Eventer. Around 65 Eventers were built (all but three were V12s and close to 50 were right-hand drive).

Poalo Gucci put his name to a $175,000/£100,000 version that must rate as the ultimate in flash, with semi-precious stones around the solid silver gear knob, fitted suitcases, a leather-bound logbook and silver ignition keys. Hmmm, tasty.

Lynx made an elegant load hauler out of the messily-designed and impractical Jaguar XJ-S. Why couldn't Jaguar have been that imaginative? Pic: Lynx Motors International

" *It was such an obvious conversion:*

it makes you wonder why Jaguar did not do it **"**

Lancia
Gamma Olgiata 1983

NUMBER BUILT: 1

For a car that led such a troubled life, the Lancia Gamma spawned a surprising number of show cars and specials. Italdesign's Megagamma Taxi was the blueprint for the first wave of multi-purpose vehicles. The T-bar equipped Gamma Spider – used by Pope John Paul II on a visit to Turin – must have been a structural nightmare because the steel-roofed production coupe was hardly a model of rigidity. The four-door, a notchback version of the coupe, was more sensible, but perhaps the most credible special-bodied Gamma was the Olgiata of 1982.

The Olgiata was an attempt by Pininfarina to revive the fortunes of Lancia's flawed Gamma range that had been plagued by technical troubles from its introduction in 1976. Based on the beautiful coupe version, the Olgiata did the rounds of motor shows in 1983, and I recall drooling over the car on the Pininfarina stand at the British show. Handsome and well balanced, it was intended to be a more upmarket interpretation of the Beta HPE and, if accepted, it might have extended the life of Lancia's flagship 2.5-litre models. Trouble was, the Gamma's fate was already sealed in 1983 when production of the saloon ceased. The one-off Olgiata gathered dust in storage for 10 years before being sold to a European collector in the mid-1990s when the Pininfarina museum decided it needed to make some space.

Would this elegant sporty estate have revived the fortunes of the Lancia Gamma? OK, probably not. Pic Pininfarina Archive

"The one-off Olgiata gathered dust in storage for 10 years"

Take a look at those heavyweight chrome bumpers ... the
Jaguar County in the 1970s, just before it was sold to an
American collector. Pic: Bob Adams

"It has now been restored (very unsympathetically considering its

historic importance, with vulgar modern seats and the like)"

Jaguar Mk II
County Estate 1960

NUMBER BUILT: 1

In the late 1950s, Jaguar works drivers Duncan Hamilton and Mike Hawthorn hatched the idea of producing an estate version of the Jaguar 3.4 saloon. They brought in racing artist Roy Nockholds to advise on the styling but before any cars were built, Hawthorn was killed in a car accident and the project was halted. When the Mk II Jaguar was announced in 1959, the idea gained new impetus and a single car was built by Jones Brothers, based on the 3.8-litre version. It had the then fashionable split tailgate arrangement, using the bottom half of the saloon bootlid (complete with a proper County badge) and a hand-made chrome-rimmed glass section. Those who recall the car say it suffered from chronic leaks and allowed fumes to be sucked into the cabin. The wooden door cappings were continued through to the luggage section. Jaguar acquired the car and used it as a service barge following the works race and rally cars around Europe. This surprisingly harmonious-looking vehicle was sold into the trade in the 1960s and ended up in America in the late 1970s. It has now been restored (very unsympathetically, considering its historic importance, with vulgar modern seats and the like) and lives in Holland.

Jaguar
Avon Stevens Estate 1980

NUMBER BUILT: UNKNOWN

Jaguar saloons have never lent themselves to estate car conversions. In the late 1950s a UK Jaguar dealer commissioned an unknown company to build a shooting brake body on the big Mk IX saloon for a customer. And there was, of course, the Mk II-based County estate (also featured in this section). Jaguar explored the possibility of an estate version of the awful XJ40 in the 1980s but thought better of it. Avon of Warwick – a company that had more famously built a drophead version of Jaguar Series II XJ coupe – converted the graceful Series III XJ into an estate in the early 1980s. The top of the body, from B-post back, was removed and the upper part of the tailgate was taken from a Renault 5. It would have set you back $15,000/£6,500 on top of the price of an XJ saloon and looked rather hearse-like at the rear. But it was, allegedly, beautifully made and second hand examples of the handful that were built are snapped up quickly. The rear seats did not fold totally flat and the fuel tanks intruded into the load space so practicality was limited.

Not the most attractive conversion, but said to be very well made, the Avon Stevens XJ would make an intriguing buy today - if you could find one. Pic: Giles Chapman Archive

"Second-hand examples of the handful that were built are snapped up quickly"

Fiat 130 Maremma
shooting brake 1974

NUMBER BUILT: 3

When the beautiful two-door coupe version of Fiat's flagship 130 range failed to boost the popularity of the car internationally, Pininfarina came up with the Maremma, a three-door estate that tapped in to the contemporary fascination with sporty load luggers. The Reliant Scimitar GTE was associated with horse-boxes and English village fetes but the Maremma was designed for the suave world of Martini-quaffing jet-setters. Pininfarina built three Maremma 130s in 1974. It was modified from the B-pillar rearwards with a hatch rear door and the rich velour of the standard coupe was replaced with a combination of Alcantara and leather. Fiat boss Gianni Agnelli, the ultimate playboy, used one of the Maremma prototypes. It did the motor show circuit in 1974 (along with a four-door version of the 130 Coupe called Opera) to great acclaim but Agnelli did not give the go-ahead for production. One Maremma sits in Pininfarina's museum and another in the hands of a private collector; the third seems to have gone missing. As well as the Maremma, there was an estate version of the 130 saloon called Villa d'Este, styled in-house by Fiat and used by various members of the Agnelli dynasty. It featured wooden side panels in the American style.

The svelte 130 Coupe made a fine basis for an sporty shooting brake. Fiat boss Gianni Agnelli liked it so much he had one built for his own use. Pic: Pininfarina Archive

"The Maremma was designed for the suave

world of Martini-quaffing jet-setters"

"It was both the fastest and most expensive estate car in the world"

Aston Martin Virage
shooting brake 1992

NUMBER BUILT: 4

There was something rather yobbish about Aston's Virage in coupe form, particularly when the shape was adorned with hot-rodder body kits and turbos, yet the estate or shooting brake version was a definite improvement. It made it seem more gentlemanly, somehow.

When the Virage shooting brake, based on Aston's big V8 Coupe, made its debut at the Geneva motor show in 1992, it was both the fastest and most expensive estate car in the world. Top speed was 152mph and and the asking price £165,000 (around a quarter of a million US dollars). Four were built (three in green) and one (in burgundy) was converted to left-hand-drive by the factory. Aston had always borrowed body furniture from lesser cars (the one-off Panelcraft DBS estate had a Hillman Hunter tailgate) so there was no shame in the Virage's Renault Savanna rear lights. It more than made up for this with a lavish interior: its detail trim and fittings were designed after consultation with Asprey, the British provider of exclusive accessories. Aston built one more Lagonda-badged four-door Virage estate but has since showed no signs of building a follow-up load carrier.

Do these men look like Aston Martin owners? We think not.
But the shooting brake looks rather better than the coupe it is
based on. Pic: Author archive

Aston Martin DB5
shooting brake 1964-67

NUMBER BUILT: 13

Five-door estate cars and three-door shooting brakes have been a minor obsession of upper-crust British marques for many years and Aston Martin was the most successful with them. The company produced a small series of cars, starting with a dozen DB5 estate cars converted by Harold Radford. His men took tin snips to the Aston's alloy roof and blended in a new panel that extended backwards to a one-piece rear door, hinged across the roof.

The suspension was firmed up at the back but otherwise the cars were mechanically stock, non-Vantage DB5s running on triple SU carburettors. These were the fastest load carriers in the world in their day ... not that a DB5 shooting brake was likely to carry 'loads' as such. A pair of Purdey shotguns, some dead game and an old copy of Country Life magazine were the heaviest items these cars were likely to haul. Curiously, the last DB5 shooting brakes were not delivered until May 1967, by which time the DB6 had been in production for almost two years. Three rather less attractive shooting brakes were built on the DB6 Mk1 chassis by FLM Panel Craft of London, with a split rear tailgate (like a Range Rover) and a more awkward side window arrangement.

The marketing team called it the fastest load carrier in the world but the DB5 shooting brake was at home in a peaceful English setting. Pic: Author archive

"*These were the fastest load carriers in the world in their day...*

not that a DB5 shooting brake was likely to carry 'loads' as such "

7

The mystique
of the 4-door

When our imaginary international man of mystery finally settled down, sired offspring and took over the family firm, he didn't necessarily want a diesel Mercedes or an Audi Station Wagon. He required a 4-door with status and glamour that could carry his family in comfort (his wife was probably a pouting countess from an exiled royal family). For just such a customer Maserati created its understated but racing-car engined Quattroporte with four camshafts, four seats and four doors. It was, with a maximum speed of 140mph, the fastest sedan in the world. Viciously expensive, it was known to few people outside its intended market yet still managed to give rise to a whole new sector populated by wannabe Quattroportes. If cars like the Iso Fidia and the De Tomaso Deauville never quite captured its essence, they still had a mystique of their own.

Iso Fidia

1969-74

NUMBER BUILT: 192

Iso was most famous for building the dramatic Grifo. But, looking at all the cars his company made, Renzo Rivolta, the boss of ISO, is most proud of the four-door Fidia.

He once told me: 'You know why? To build a four-door that performs like a Grifo is more difficult than to build a sports car. And I really like the idea of having good performance plus the space to put everything I need in the car. I had a Grifo for six months and I couldn't fit anything – not even my dog – so I decided I had to build a bigger car. I was very proud of that car. It was very modern: you see the new Cadillac, even the Jaguars – they're very similar. The Maserati Quattroporte was a bit bulky, a heavy car not nice to drive. My idea was to have a four-door you can drive like a Grifo.'

But it wasn't a success, I suggested. 'Not many were made. I realised it was a mistake because a lot of customers for the four-door Fidia expected it to be a Mercedes. Expectations are higher with saloons and the end of the story is that it costs more to make, but you get less money because people pay more for a sports car than a saloon. So financially it was too exclusive.' But not so for Beatle John Lennon who bought one.

Glamorous and sophisticated as it was, the styling of the Fidia never quite came together and it tempted few buyers away from their Mercedes and Maseratis. Pic: Jason Yorke Edgill

"I really like the idea of having good performance

plus the space to put everything I need in the car"

David Brown liked his Lagondas, and the four-door version of the DBS V8 was really designed to placate the boss, but few customers felt the need to buy one. Pic: Author archive

"*It was not an especially happy-looking car*"

Aston Martin Lagonda

NUMBER BUILT: 7

William Towns joined Aston Martin as a seat designer but soon made it known that he would like to be a stylist. Towns, who had worked at Rover on the Rover-BRM Gas Turbine Racer and before that at Rootes, put together some sketches of how he saw the next generation of Aston Martins developing. One was a broad, squat two-door car that would eventually emerge in production as the DBS while the other was a four-door long-wheelbase Lagonda version of the same basic design.

Aston Martin boss David Brown approved Towns' designs and both were signed off in 1966. There was no time or money to put the four-door into production, mainly because of problems with Aston's new V8 engine, and a downturn in Brown's core tractor business. So the Lagonda idea was shelved, apart from a 1969 one-off with a new V8 injection engine, built for David Brown. As Aston Martin desperately looked for ways to drum up new business, the four-door Lagonda idea was revived. The Lagonda displayed at the London Motor Show in 1974 had been stretched by 12 inches and it was not an especially happy looking car. Its cause was not helped by the rather Edsel-like front grille and by the time Aston went into liquidation not long afterwards, only seven Lagondas had been built. Aston Martin is now part of Ford Motor Company.

Maserati Quattroporte
1963-70

NUMBER BUILT: 679

The Maserati Quattroporte, styled by Frua, was Italy's answer to the big Jaguars of the day and represented the ultimate in speed and luxury in the saloon class. The shape was assertive and dignified, if not quite beautiful. This four-door Maserati attracted a number of celebrities, including actors Stewart Grainger and Laurence Harvey. There was beauty to be found under the bonnet in the form of Maserati's four-camshaft 4.2-litre V8 engine, which was possessed of great smoothness and torque. In manual form the Quattroporte could touch 140mph with the ZF five-speed manual transmission, and this made it the world's fastest saloon car.

The cars built before 1965 featured square headlamps and a DeDion rear axle, but later versions had four headlamps and a beam axle. Interiors were also more luxurious on later cars but all came with equipment including electric windows (a rarity in the 1960s), and many had air conditioning. A few were built with the 4.7-litre V8 engine. Maserati built 679 Quattroportes but many were chopped up to build replicas of the manufacturer's 450S.

The original four-door supercar had presence and panache even if it lacked true beauty. Pic: Author archive.

"*The shape was assertive and dignified, if not quite beautiful*"

Maserati Quattroporte

A natural sucessor to the original 1963-70 Quattroporte, this clean-lined design was overlooked for the fussy Bertone design of the Quattroporte II. Pic: BillMcGrath Maserati/Bruce Milner

"The Aga Khan bought the first Frua prototype and eventually gave it to his favourite jockey "

Frua sedan

NUMBER BUILT: 2

Maserati was bought by Citroen in the late 1960s but had it remained independent, the Quattroporte Frua would have been the replacement for the Quattroporte that had been selling quite well since 1963. When the final first series QPs were sold in 1970, Maserati's Pietro Frua was working on this glassy handsome saloon as a replacement. He based it on the 2+2 Indy GT chassis that was effectively much the same as the old Quattroporte, with a solid rear axle and a 4.7-litre V8.

The Frua sedan was displayed at the Geneva show in 1972 but, by then, Maserati management had decided to pursue the Citroen SM-based Quattroporte II that proved deeply unpopular and was soon dropped. The Aga Khan bought the first Frua prototype and eventually gave it to his favourite jockey; a second was sold to King Juan Carlos of Spain.

When the original Quattroporte was announced, there had been no other truly exotic super saloons but, as the 1970s dawned, the market was getting crowded. There were challengers from Iso, Monteverdi and an upstart called the Monica from France, but Ferrari and Lamborghini never built a car in this sector. Citroen sold Maserati to De Tomaso in the mid-1970s, and Fiat acquired the brand as a partner for Ferrari in the early 1990s.

Lagonda Rapide

NUMBER BUILT: 55

In the early 1960s, Aston Martin was determined to produce a high-class saloon that would rival the products of Rolls-Royce. The model given that job was the Lagonda Rapide, which was intended as a car for the wealthy who occasionally enjoyed driving themselves. The Rapide appeared at European motor shows in 1961, and had two important features never seen on production Aston Martins. The Rapide was powered by a 4-litre version of the straight-six engine (for more torque at low speeds) and a Dedion rear axle, which theoretically gave a better ride and took up less luggage space.

The styling, by Touring of Milan, was wrought in alloy and proved controversial due to its horseshoe grille and fussy, twin headlights with an angled brow above them. It was a shame, because from the back the Rapide was an elegant car. It was capable of 125mph but at the price (more than $14,000/£5,000) there were better luxury saloons and few potential buyers could get on with the styling. The car was unpopular within the company as it was time-consuming to build and took labour away from the construction of the DB4 for which demand far outstripped supply. Of the 55 Rapides that were built, many were sold to rich friends of Aston Martin boss David Brown.

Apart from its Ford Edsel-like front end, the Rapide was a handsome, powerful looking saloon built on the insistence of David Brown.
Pic: Author archive

"The car was unpopular within the company as it was time-consuming to build and took labour away from the construction of the DB4"

Was it a coincidence the Deauville looked so much like an XJ6? Unlikely, but it was still a cool car and one that earned owners respect wherever they drove it. Pic: Jon Antonaki

De Tomaso Deauville
1970-88

NUMBER BUILT: 355

The Deauville, a large four-door saloon, was De Tomaso's challenge to the Jaguar XJ6. In fact, it looked so similar you wonder how he ever avoided a lawsuit. Designed by Tom Tjaarda, an American working for Ghia, the Deauville used Ford Mustang engines (although the prototype had a special overhead-cam Ford V8), and many other components from the American manufacturer. Early cars, while sumptuously trimmed in soft Italian leathers and suedes, sported hideous plasticky steering wheels straight from a 1970s Ford gas-guzzler.

Only 355 Deauvilles were made, between 1970 and 1988, and one was bought by British advertising executive Charles Saatchi, an international art collector. They were quick cars with good handling, but they never attained the levels of sophistication in terms of build quality and refinement expected of even mass-produced rivals. De Tomaso built a special Deauville station wagon for his wife, but his most famous car remains the Pantera, a mid-engined slingshot that looked set for widespread American success until it was dropped unceremoniously by its sponsor, Ford.

Monteverdi 375/4

NUMBER BUILT: 7

The deliciously obscure and glamorous Monteverdi cars from Switzerland seemed to be from another dimension, the kind of machinery people in the Martini ads drove. They were designed for well-groomed jet setters who never caught colds or ironed their own shirts. And I nearly bought one that was sitting in the front garden of a house in Bath in southern England.

The 375/4 was not so much an alpine Ferrari, more a kind of Swiss Jensen. These big cars combined massive urge (from a Chrysler 7.2-litre V8) with a svelte and luxurious GT body styled by Frua (with help from Peter Monteverdi himself, or so he claimed). The bodywork was built in Italy by Fissore, in which Monteverdi later took a 50 per cent stake, and the cars were put together behind the showrooms in Basle.

To lovers of exotic saloons, the 375/4 is the ultimate Monteverdi. Based on the chassis of his 375L coupe, Peter Monteverdi let 26 inches into the wheelbase to give his flagship saloon fantastic leg-stretching room in the back, where tycoons could enjoy the air conditioning or watch their favourite programmes on a built-in TV set. The 375/4 was one of the fastest four-door cars in the world and also one of the rarest (only seven were built). Monteverdi hoped to sell the cars to the Swiss government but it stuck with Mercedes. Some 375/4 Monteverdis were sold to the King of Qatar.

*The 375/4 Monteverdi mixed limousine-like scale with sports car
proportions but didn't find much favour in the VIP market ...
even with a TV in the back as standard. Pic: Jason Yorke Edgill*

" *The 375/4 was one of the fastest four-door cars*

in the world and also one of the rarest **"**

> *"The car was under-powered, weighing 500lb*
>
> *more than the already corpulent SM"*

Maserati

MASERATI
quattro porte II

Quattroporte II
1974-77

NUMBER BUILT: 5

Maserati enjoyed modest success with its original Quattroporte V8 of 1963 but the replacement, in the form of the Quattroporte II, did not appear until 1974. This was to be the final product of the company's patchy association with Citroen. Under the fussy and rather undistinguished Bertone-styled body – from the pen of Marcello Gandini, father of the Lamborghini Countach, among many other more memorable cars – lurked the drivetrain of the Citroen SM (a 3-litre V6 and a front-wheel-drive five-speed transaxle). The car was under powered, weighing 500lb more than the already corpulent SM, but owners enjoyed a good ride from the Citroen-derived suspension and an opulent leather-trimmed cabin. Just as the car was coming to fruition, Citroen terminated its ownership of Maserati and the QP II was left in limbo. Maserati's new owner (De Tomaso) did not want any part of such a complex Citroen-based design and the French wanted to wipe their hands of anything associated with the SM project. De Tomaso scrapped the last few hundred SM bodyshells rather than build complete cars that few people wanted to buy after the 1970s fuel crisis. In the end, at least five Quattroporte IIs were sold (some say it was as many as 13), split between favoured Arab and Spanish customers.

Only five of these were built yet Maserati had high enough
hopes to produce a brochure. The styling didn't work and with a
mere V6 engine, the QP II was rather over weight.
Pic: Author archive

Maserati
Quattroporte III 1978-90

NUMBER BUILT: 2,100

When Alejandro De Tomaso took over Maserati, he believed there was still a demand for a large V8 four-door, despite the failure of the V6 model. So, using the Maserati Kyalami as a platform, he commissioned ItalDesign to build an angular and imposing sedan in the tradition of the original Quattroporte with a truly lavish interior. De Tomaso's hunch proved correct and following warm press reviews, the new Quattroporte became Maserati's best-seller within two years. It enjoyed a 12-year production run and was the last of the traditionally built big Maseratis powered by the four-camshaft V8 engine, first as a 4.2-litre, later a 4.9. Most were automatic but a manual gearbox was optional. The Middle East market took many of the cars, usually in white with white leather, which was quite an eyeful. The last 55 cars were built to special order and badged Royale, with interiors featuring walnut writing tables and pewter goblets. In April 1986, at the Turin motor show, a one-off Quattroporte limousine was displayed with a wheelbase 2ft longer than standard, and a higher roofline. The front passenger seat was rotatable, and equipment included a video recorder with monitor, special sound system, foldaway tables and air conditioning with separate temperature controls for the rear passengers. In the 1980s, Italian president Sandro Pertini favoured a Maserati Quattroporte saloon and famously upset Enzo Ferrari when he used the car on a visit to Maranello, home of Ferrari.

"The Middle East market took many of the cars, usually in

white with white leather, which was quite an eyeful "

The Quattroporte III emphasized oppulence as much as speed and was the last Maserati to use the quad-cam V8 engine. It also looked a bit like an overgrown mini-cab. Pic; John Antonaki

8

Call the taste police

This chapter is the antidote to the rest of the book. It is a distillation of some of the world's rarest and most vulgar luxury cars, built to service the needs of a certain kind of rich person so sated by life's finer things that they can no longer identify where luxury ends and vulgarity begins. Few marques are immune to this sad phenomenon – you'll find Rolls-Royce, Lagonda and even Bugatti represented here. But it is really a celebration of the gold-plated world of the neo-classic, a genre invented by Americans in the 1960s when several revered but defunct pre-war names were exhumed and reinterpreted in the modern idiom, rather in the manner of Led Zeppelin doing Beethoven. Think K-tel *Hooked on Classics*. Think porn stars, bad actors and anybody with more money than taste having a mid-life crisis, wearing a jumpsuit and blasting out their greatest hits in Vegas.

Excalibur
1965 to date

NUMBER BUILT: UNKNOWN

Only those with a strong sense of the ironic could entertain the idea of an Excalibur. Dubbed a 'neo classic' by its American makers, the first examples were built in the early 1960s and soon became the required transport for flamboyant Hollywood film producers and other showbiz types bored with the usual European status symbol cars.

The Excalibur, designed by Brook Stevens, was no cheap kit-car: based on a massive separate chassis (originally a Studebaker design), it had a high-quality GRP (glass-reinforced plastic) body shaped in the image of a 1920s Mercedes SSK roadster, complete with functional exhaust headers. Corvette engines of 5.3 litres and later 7.0 litres were used, usually with automatic transmission. The1965 and 1966 models were roadsters, but the four-seater Phaeton became optional from 1967. They still make Excaliburs today: California Governor Arnie Schwarzenegger has one and Tommy Steele (dubbed Britain's first rock 'n' roll star) was an owner until recently. The Excalibur was the transport of America's answer to James Bond, Derek Flint, as played with tongue firmly in cheek by James Coburn in *Our Man Flint* and *In Like Flint*.

What can we say? The Excalibur exceeds normal parameters of bad taste and enters a new dimension. Pic: Bob Adams

"*They still make Excaliburs today:*

California Governor Arnie Schwarzenegger has one"

JOK 568N

BUGATTI

PROTOTIPO SU AUTOTELAIO

ORIGINALE BUGATTI 101-c.

" *The 101 was a fine car but totally outdated in the post-war market* "

Bugatti 101C

1965

NUMBER BUILT: 1

Six Bugatti 101Cs were built in 1951 when the car made its debut at the Paris motor show. A warmed-over T57 with a straight-eight engine and a beam front axle, the 101 was a fine car but totally outdated in the post-war market. By then Bugatti was on its last legs and had lost the will to live. Only five of the cars were bodied, mostly as rather sober saloons and cabriolets. The sixth chassis languished at the Bugatti factory until it was bought by Scott Bailey, an American who later sold the car to former Chrysler stylist Virgil Exner for $7,000/£2,500. Exner was in the midst of his 'revival cars' period; he had created a range of neo-classics, mostly based on contemporary American running gear, in an attempt to resuscitate marques like Duesenberg, Packard and Mercer. Returning to a theme he had started on his Mercer Cobra, Exner rebodied the Bugatti in his contemporary retro-modern style, blending the traditional Bugatti radiator with a muscular roadster body. This had a massive front overhang but a rather stunted wheelbase as the chassis had been shortened by 18 inches. It was entirely outrageous and appalled Bugatti enthusiasts but Exner retained his 101C until his death in 1973 when it had done only 1,000 miles.

It's Batmobile meets The Munsters and another starring role for those Renault 16 headlights. The Type 101C was truly an outrage – yet wonderful.

*Straight from the set of the TV series UFO, the Owen Sedanca
should only be driven while wearing a beige jumpsuit and
blonde wig. Underneath lurks a humble XJ6 Jaguar.*
Pic: Dermot Healy

"Eighty orders were taken ... but these soon evaporated as

the grim reality of the fuel crisis became more evident "

Owen Sedanca

NUMBER BUILT: 3

To the child of the 1970s, the Owen Sedanca looks like a car sketched on the front of a book during a particularly dull maths lesson. Long, low and dramatic, it has the futuristic appeal of a car built as a prop for a sci-fi film, driven by a character in a beige jumpsuit and a blond wig. The Sedanca might have achieved modest success, but within days of its launch in September 1973, the market for large, luxurious cars collapsed as the fuel crisis began to take hold. The Owen Sedanca was a coachbuilt Jaguar XJ6 commissioned by HR Owen, Rolls-Royce dealers in Britain, and production was overseen by a 23-year-old designer called Chris Humberstone. A complete XJ6 was bought, HR Owen's parts bins raided for any additional items and the entire XJ body removed and replaced with Humberstone's aluminium-panelled wedge-profiled coupe.

Eighty orders were taken at the car's London Kensington unveiling but these soon evaporated as the grim reality of the fuel crisis became more evident. Jaguar's refusal to give the project its blessing seemed to put the final nails in its coffin. Two further cars were commissioned in bizarre circumstances. A man ordered a Sedanca for his son to use within the grounds of his large Oxfordshire estate (it was built by Panther in 1978). When the man's younger son saw the car, he wanted one, so a second Sedanca was ordered but not completed until 1983.

Daimler 104
Ladies Model 1955

NUMBER BUILT: 50

In the days when women of a certain social standing were only meant to be decorative creatures with three-inch waistlines, large hats and long white gloves, Daimler produced its idea of their ideal car. Enter, in 1955, the 104 Ladies Model. Almost certainly inspired by Lady Docker (the colourful wife of company boss Sir Bernard Docker), it came complete with fitted umbrella, a coloured and sectioned map (just in case the poor things got lost), a vanity case for cosmetic emergencies and a travel rug. Other 1955 Ladies Model items included an ice flask, shooting stick, picnic hamper, electric windows and four fitted suitcases. And because no woman could possibly keep in her pretty little head what all those switches and levers were for, each one was labelled. The Ladies Model was based on the 104, so called because it would do an alleged 104mph. By the spring of 1956 the car had been discontinued as a distinct model and the special ladies' items became extras. Today, only one complete Ladies Model 104 is known to the Daimler and Lanchester Owners Club.

Move over darlng ... the man at the wheel in this marketing artist's impression hasn't realised the lady should be driving. Pic: Author archive

"It came complete with fitted umbrella and a coloured

and sectioned map (just in case the poor things got lost)"

Duesenberg II

NUMBER BUILT: 1

In the 1920s and '30s, Duesenberg built what many regarded as America's finest cars. This wild limousine was an attempt to revive the name and had been preceded by a one-off coupe on a 1950 Packard chassis (powered by an original straight-eight Duesenberg engine) which, presumably, had been its inspiration. Designed by the former Chrysler stylist Virgil Exner, it was at the time said to be the largest 'production' car in the world, with more headroom and legroom than any American car. The boot was the biggest, too.

The styling mixed old and new to produce a car that looked like something the Adams Family should have been driving around in. Ghia of Italy built the body and Chrysler supplied the power, a 425bhp 7-litre V8. At $19,500/£7,000, it came fully loaded with every conceivable feature you could have imagined in 1966 – even an auto pilot. It's not clear exactly what this was, but it might have been an early form of electronic assistance that put the brakes on when you were travelling too close to the car in front. Elvis Presley and Jerry Lewis had their names down for the first production cars but the single prototype was seized by US marshals when it was found that Duesenberg had failed to pay its salesmen commission.

The car with everything and it should have been a big sales success ... trouble was that Duesenberg failed to pay its salesmen money they were owed. Pic: Classic Cars

"*The styling mixed old and new to produce a car that looked like something the Adams Family should have been driving around in* "

Panther De Ville

NUMBER BUILT: 60

The Panther De Ville came to encapsulate everything that was ostentatious about the 1970s. It was conceived by Robert Jankel to appease a growing band of wealthy clients with more money than taste: singer Sir Elton John and actor Oliver Reed were noted buyers. Purists sneered but Jankel sat back and reeled in the cash. Sitting on a massive 142in wheelbase, the tubular-framed De Ville used a Jaguar 6- or (much more commonly) 12-cylinder engine. With its flowing winglines and big headlights, it was styled to ape the massive straight-eight engined 1930 Bugatti Royale of which six were built.

The Panther De Ville was equipped with Jaguar suspension, power steering and automatic transmission, so it was an easy car to drive and quite quick, although poor aerodynamics tended to keep the top speed low. Interiors were lavish and often featured TV sets and drinks bars. About 60 De Villes were hand-built between 1974 and 1985, including seven two-door convertibles (for many years Britain's most expensive listed production car), and one pink and gold six-door limousine. The car came to prominence again in the most recent version of 101 Dalmatians (fittingly, it was Cruella DeVille's car). As the original Jaguar engine was not up to the rigours of stunt driving, it was replaced with a small-block Chevrolet V8. Eagle-eyed anoraks will have spotted the unlikely origins of the De Ville's front doors: an unglamorous British car from the 1960s, the BMC 1800.

Straight out of the world of a soft-porn film, the Panther De Ville was not for shrinking violets. Pic: John Antonaki

"It was styled to ape the massive straight-eight

engined 1930 Bugatti Royale of which six were built"

Panther J72

1972-81

NUMBER BUILT: 426

In America, flamboyant movie stars and other glitterati drove revived Stutz cars or perhaps an Excalibur: Britain had the Panther J72. Robert Jankel, former fashion designer and textile tycoon, built the first Panther J72 in 1972, and it was a Jaguar-powered copy of the 1930s SS100 Jaguar sports car. Jankel wanted an original Jaguar SS100 but, when he discovered how much they cost, he decided to build his own. It was based on Jaguar hardware with XJ suspension, 6- or 12-cylinder engines and manual or automatic transmission. The J72 was pretty dreadful but it was beautifully made and, in V12-form, frighteningly fast with a top speed of 130mph when the brick-like aerodynamics started to take effect. Presumably, if you got enough wind underneath those big front wings, the J72 would eventually lift-off. Owners included actress Elizabeth Taylor and Frederick *Day of the jackal* Forsyth. Panther made a surprising number of J72s but dropped the model to concentrate on the much cheaper, higher-volume Lima and its successor, the Kallista. Today Jankel no longer builds Panthers (he sold the name to a Korean company in the 1980s) but continues in the motor trade, building armoured cars and various one-off or very low-volume projects for special clients.

A modern interpretation of a Jaguar SS100, the Panther J72
sold in surprisingly large numbers to people who wanted old
car looks with modern go. Pic: John Antonaki

Rolls-Royce
Camargue 1975-86

NUMBER BUILT: 534

The Pininfarina-styled Camargue, Rolls-Royce's flamboyant 1970s super coupe, was a car for kings, princes, diplomats and superstars: a hedonistic two-door with no true rival. There was little to match the Camargue for size in the coupe stakes and nothing on price. The Camargue was the most expensive car in America at its launch in 1976, costing 50 per cent more than even a RR Corniche convertible. In Britain, it outshone the massive Phantom VI, then a mere £21,000/$30,000. Over the course of 11 years, Rolls-Royce built 534 Camargues but never completed more than one a week. Each car took six months to assemble.

Unsurprisingly, the Camargue's best market was the USA, followed by its native Britain (where Welsh singer Shirley Bassey and blue comedian Bernard Manning were among the buyers) and then Saudi Arabia.

The 120mph Camargue was the first Rolls-Royce to have curved window glass and first to be designed to metric dimensions. The car used a slightly more powerful 6.7-litre alloy Rolls pushrod V8 allied to the GM three-speed automatic gearbox, with Rolls' usual independent suspension. The superb split-level air-conditioning system on the $47,000/£29,000 Camargue cost as much as a Mini car and had the cooling capacity of 30 domestic refrigerators.

In the 1970s, the Bentley Continental R was Rolls' brave and effective replacement, and after three years of production had outsold the Camargue, proving the original design approach was right.

In standard form the Camargue had a certain presence (above) but it all went badly wrong when the customisers got hold of one (left) for someone with more money than taste.
Pics: Pininfarina Archive and Frank Dale & Stepsons

"*There was little to match the Camargue for size in the coupe stakes and nothing on price*"

Stutz Blackhawk
1970-93

NUMBER BUILT: UNKNOWN

Like the Excalibur, the Stutz (a revival of an old American name last seen in the 1930s) was a vulgar car for the American showbiz aristocracy in the briefly fashionable 'neo classic' mould, blending pre-war and contemporary styling to frankly outrageous effect. As well as the Blackhawk coupe you could have a Bearcat convertible, a Victoria sedan or a huge Royale state limo.

Elvis Presley bought the first Blackhawk from under the nose of Frank Sinatra on a live TV show and went on to add three more to his collection. Boxers Larry Holmes and Muhammad Ali and entertainers Liberace, Dean Martin and Kenny Rogers were all proud Stutz owners. The car was also popular with Arab rulers like King Fahd of Saudi Arabia and the Sultan of Brunei. Stutz cars were based around the Pontiac Grand Prix, with the bodies refashioned in Italy by Carrozzeria Padama to Exner's design. Ghia built the first prototype and early versions had a huge 7-litre engine with as much as 430bhp in pre-emission form, but the 1970s Middle East fuel crisis caused a gas-saving power drop to pitiful levels, as it did with all big American engines. The Stutz possibly eclipses the Panther De Ville as the ultimate in bad taste and yet it remains strangely fascinating.

"The Stutz possibly eclipses the Panther De Ville as the ultimate in bad taste"

It's another flight of fancy from Mr Exner ... the Stutz is wonderfully camp and should only be driven with tongue firmly in cheek. Pic: Frank Dale & Stepsons

Aston Martin 1983–90
Lagonda Tickford

NUMBER BUILT: UNKNOWN

It is hard to over emphasise the impact of the wedge-shaped Aston Martin Lagonda at the London Motor Show in 1976, when around 250 enthusiasts were impressed enough to pay deposits that hauled Aston Martin back from the brink of yet another bankruptcy. Styled by William Towns, the Lagonda took seven months from sketch to prototype and drew huge publicity for its solid-state gas plasma instrument display and touch-sensitive controls, as well as for its sharp-edged look. Hand-built in alloy on the existing Aston V8 hardware, it was three years before the first cars were delivered, at double the original price, and even then there were problems with the over ambitious electronics.

Originally, the Lagonda appealed to the aristocracy. Lord and Lady Tavistock bought the first one (which broke down in front of the assembled world's press), and the Duke of Westminster was stopped for speeding in his. From 1983, the Tickford version of the Lagonda was festooned with spoilers and TV sets, and finished entirely in white, making it the ultimate car for speed-loving oil sheikhs. The original shape resisted all attempts to 'improve' it and the softened series IV version was ruined at the skin-lines stage – and was nothing like Towns had envisaged it.

William Towns' Lagonda had lost whatever dignity it possessed with the Tickford version – the pictures reveal all. Most of them went to the Middle East and hopefully won't return to Britain.
Pic John Antonaki

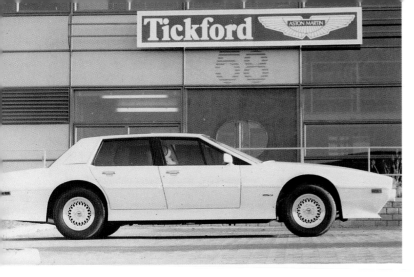

Acknowledgements

The pictures in this book are at least as important as the words, and the rarity of

some of the cars required a widespread search for a suitable image. My thanks go to all

who helped, but most especially to Giles Chapman, Julian Nowill, Pictorial Press,

DaimlerChrysler Archive, Pininfarina Archive, Gus Gregory, Jason Yorke-Edgill, John

Mayston-Taylor and *Classic Cars* magazine.

Martin Buckley
January 2004

Index

250 California Spider, 89
328GTB, 128
330GTC, 89
500 Superfast Series, 89
8-litre Bentley, 5, 41, 42, 43
Adenauer, Chancellor Konrad, 35
Aga Khan, 80, 171
Agnelli, Gianni, 86, 156
Agnelli, Giovanni, 44
Alfa 166, 19
Alfa Romeo, 78
Ali, Muhammad, 200
AMC Pacer, 141
AMG CL65, 134, 135
Amin, Idi, 23
Artioli, Romano, 132
Aston DB4 GT, 97
Aston Martin, 148, 172
Aston Martin DB4 GT Zagato, 108, 109
Aston Martin DB5, 160, 161
Aston Martin Lagonda Tickford, 202, 203
Aston Martin Lagonda, 166, 167
Aston Martin V12 Lagonda, 41
Aston Martin V8 Zagato, 106, 107
Aston Martin Virage, 158, 159
Atkinson, Rowan, 106
Audi 100, 14
Audi A8, 23
Audi Station Wagon, 163
Automobile Shippers Inc., 70
Avon of Warwick, 154
Bailey, Scott, 187
Baker, Ginger, 83
Bardot, Brigitte, 77
Barnato, Woolf, 42
Bassey, Shirley, 198
Bearcat convertible, 200
Beethoven, 183
Benny, Jack, 46

Bentley 8-litre, 5, 41, 42, 43
Bentley Continental GT, 135
Bentley Continental R, 198
Bentley Cresta, 44, 45
Bentley, W. O., 42, 60
Bertone, 80, 98, 119
Beta HPE (Lancia), 150
Biarritz convertible, 55
Bizzarrini GT Strada, 104, 105
Bizzarrini, Giotto, 105
BMC, 146
BMW, 119, 127
BMW 505, 34, 35
BMW 6-Series, 102
BMW 7-Series, 23
BMW CSL coupe, 102
BMW M1, 102, 103
BMW-Glas 3000, 72
Bond, James, 110, 184
Bristol 407 Viotti Convertible, 92, 93
Brown, David, 167, 172
Bugatti 101C, 186, 187
Bugatti EB110, 132, 133
Bugatti Royale, 7, 8, 9, 194
Bugatti, 123, 183
Bugatti, Ettore 7
Buick, 11
Cadillac, 23, 30, 41, 64, 164
Cadillac Eldorado Brougham Jacqueline
Coupe, 54, 55
Cadillac Eldorado Brougham, 41
Cadillac Eldorado Brougham, 52, 53
Canadian War Museum, 20
Canberra, 27
Carrozzeria Padama, 200
Chaika-Gaz 13, 10, 11
Changchun No 1 Automobile Factory, 16
Chapron, Henri, 12
Chrysler Ghia L 6.4, 70, 71

Chrysler, 41, 46, 84, 91, 113, 176, 187, 192
Citroen CX Prestige Turbo, 12
Citroen DS, 12, 14
Citroen SM Chapron, 12, 13
Citroen, 100, 171, 179
Coburn, James, 184
Cold War, 11, 30
Cooper, Gary, 50
Cord 812 Supercharged Sportsman, 100, 101
Cord, E. L., 50
Corvette (Chevrolet), 119, 184
Coupe Napoleon, 8
Crook, Tony, 93
Crown Imperial Ghia Limousines, 46, 47
Crown Prince Akihito, 39
CSL coupe (BMW), 102
Curtis, Tony, 91
Cussler, Clive, 49
CX Prestige Turbo (Citroen), 12
Daimler 104 Ladies Model, 190, 191
Daimler and Lanchester Owners Club, 190
Daimler Straight-eight 'Green Goddess', 41,
    48, 49
Daimler-Benz, 20
Daninos, Jean, 44, 91
de Gaulle, Charles, 14
De Tomaso Deauville, 163, 174, 175
De Tomaso Pantera, 175
De Tomaso, 171, 179
De Tomaso, Alejandro, 180
di Montezemolo, Luca, 136
Dodge Firearrow, 70
Duesenberg, 41, 187
Duesenberg II, 192, 193
Duesenberg SJ, 50, 51
Duesenberg, Fred and August, 50
Edsel, 63
Ekland, Britt, 93
Eldorado Brougham (Cadillac), 41

Elysée Palace, 12
Emperor Hirohito, 23
Excalibur, 184, 185, 197, 200
Exner, Virgil, 70, 187, 192
Facel Vega Excellence, 14, 15
Facel Vega Facel II, 90, 91
Facel Vega, 44, 75
Fangio, Juan Manuel, 139
Ferguson, Harry, 83
Ferrari, 77, 119, 123, 132, 171, 176
Ferrari 250 (GT) SWB, 108
Ferrari 250 California Spider, 89
Ferrari 250LM, 105
Ferrari 328 GTB, 128
Ferrari 330 GTC, 89
Ferrari 365 California Spider, 88, 89
Ferrari 400 Superamerica, 86, 87
Ferrari 410, 84, 85
Ferrari 500 Superfast Series, 89, 94, 95
Ferrari Enzo, 5, 19, 78, 94, 129, 136, 137
Ferrari F40, 128, 129
Ferrari F50, 130, 131
Ferrari Superamerica S1, 2 & 3, 84, 85, 89
Fiat, 44, 171
Fiat 130 Maremma, 141, 156, 157
Fiat 2300S Coupe, 70
Fiat 8V, 98, 99
Fiat Otto Vu, 98
Fiat Uno, 139
Fiat-Lancia, 114
Fissore, 176
Flint, Derek, 184
FLM Panel Craft of London, 160
Ford Anglia, 56
Ford Edsel, 173
Ford GT40, 105
Ford Mk II, 63
Ford MkII Granada Ghia X, 4
Ford Motor Company, 167
Ford Mustang, 175
Ford, 119
Formula One, 128, 131, 136
Forsyth, Frederick, 197
Frua, 80, 168, 176
Gable, Clark, 50
Gamma Spider (Lancia), 150
Gandini, Marcello, 132, 179
Garbo, Greta, 50

Gardner, Ava, 14
Gasaroll, Gene, 70
General Franco, 24, 78
Geneva Motor Show, 36, 98, 159, 171
Ghia Coupe, 84
Ghia Dart, 70
Ghia of Turin, 46
Ghia, 41, 98, 175, 192, 200
Ghia-Aigle of Switzerland, 35
Giacosa, Dante, 98
Glas V8, 72, 73
Glas, Hans, 72
Glaserati, 72
Goggomobile, 72
Good, Alan, 60
Gorbeachev, Mikhail, 30, 32
Graber Alvis, 74, 75
Graber, Hermann, 75
Graf Zeppelin airships, 69
Grainger, Stewart, 168
Grand Prix, 102
Gucci, Poalo, 148
Hamilton, Duncan, 153
Harrison, George, 127
Harvey, Laurence, 168
Hawthorn, Mike, 153
Hemi engine, 113
Hitler, Adolf, 20, 23, 64
Hoare, Col. Ronnie, 94
Holmes, Larry, 200
Hong-Qi Red Flag, 4, 5, 7, 16, 17
Humberstone, Chris, 189
Hurst, William Randolph, 50
Integrale EVO (Lancia), 114
Invicta Black Prince, 56, 57
Iso Fidia, 163, 164, 165
Iso Grifo 7-litre, 118, 119
Iso Grifo, 105
Isotta Fraschini Monterosa, 58, 59
ItalDesign, 180
Jaguar 3.4 saloon, 153
Jaguar Avon Stevens Estate, 141, 154, 155
Jaguar E-type, 91
Jaguar Mk II County Estate, 141, 152, 153
Jaguar Series II XJ coupe, 154
Jaguar SS100, 197
Jaguar XJ40, 154
Jaguar XJ6, 175, 189

Jaguar XKSS, 97, 116, 117
Jaguar, 56, 148, 164, 194
Jankel, Robert, 194, 197
Jaray, Paul, 69
Jensen FF (Ferguson Formula), 82, 83
John, Sir Elton, 194
Johnson, Lyndon B., 46
Jones Brothers, 153
Kennedy, Jacqueline, 55
Kennedy, John F., 46
King Fahd of Saudi Arabia, 200
King Juan Carlos of Spain, 171
King of Qatar, 176
King Zog, 7
Koot, Paul, 114
Lady Docker, 190
Lagonda Rapide, 172, 173
Lagonda V12, 60, 61
Lagonda, 183
Lamborghini Countach, 179
Lamborghini LM 002, 142, 143
Lamborghini Miura, 113
Lamborghini, 4, 102, 132, 171
Lampredi, Aurelio, 59
Lancia Flaminia 335 'Quirinale', 19
Lancia Gamma Olgiata, 150, 151
Lancia Gamma Spider, 150
Lancia Hyena, 114, 115
Lancia Integrale EVO, 114
Lancia Kappa saloons, 19
Lancia Megagamma Taxi, 150
Lauda, Niki, 102
Le Mans 24-hour race, 124, 127
Led Zeppelin, 183
Ledwinka, Hans, 36
Legachev, Yegor Ligachev, 30
Lennon, John, 164
Lewis, Jerry, 192
Liberace, 200
Lincoln Continental II, 41, 62, 63
London Motor Show, 49, 60, 94, 167, 202
Lotus Elan, 91, 127
Lucas, Chris Keith, 148
Lynx Eventer, 148, 149
Manning, Bernard, 198
Martin, Dean, 70, 200
Maserati 5000GT, 80 81
Maserati Kyalami, 180

Maserati Quattroporte Frua Sedan, 170, 171
Maserati Quattroporte II, 178, 179
Maserati Quattroporte III, 180, 181
Maserati Quattroporte, 19, 163, 164, 168, 169
Maserati, 12, 77, 132
Maserati, Ghibli, 119
Maybach DS-8 Zeppelin, 68, 69
McLaren F1, 126, 127, 135, 136
McLaren, 123
McQueen, Steve, 116
Megagamma Taxi (Lancia), 150
Mercedes 300, 35
Mercedes 540K Special Roadster, 64, 65
Mercedes 600 Pullman, 22, 23
Mercedes 600, 14
Mercedes C111 Rotary, 120, 121
Mercedes CL Coupe, 135
Mercedes S-Class, 23
Mercedes, 7, 28, 32, 69, 91, 123, 162, 164, 176
Mercedes, SSK, 184
Mercedes-Benz Argentina, 139
Mercedes-Benz CLK GTR, 124, 125
Mercedes-Benz Grosser, 20, 21
Mercer, 187
MG Rover, 146
MG TC, 24
Michelotti, Giovanni, 35
Mini, 198
Mitterand, Francois, 12
Montand, Yves, 44
Monteverdi 375/4, 176, 177
Monteverdi Hai, 97, 112, 113
Monteverdi, 4, 5, 171
Monteverdi, Peter, 113, 176
Morro, Aldo, 19
Murray, Gordon, 127
Nissan Prince Royal Limousine, 38, 39
Nissan, 110
Nockholds, Roy, 153
Otto Vu (Fiat), 98
Owen Sedanca, 188, 189
Packard Caribbean, 11
Packard, 30, 187, 192
Pagani Zonda C12S, 138, 139
Pagani, Horacio, 139
Pantera (De Tomaso), 175
Panther De Ville, 194, 195, 200
Panther J72, 196, 197

Panther, 189
Paris Motor Show, 44, 75
Pegaso Z102/Z103, 78, 79
Pertini, Sandro, 180
Pertini, Sandro, 19
Pininfarina Coupe Aerodynamico, 86
Pininfarina Superfast, 84
Pininfarina, 19, 39, 44, 55, 80, 95, 98, 131,
150, 156, 198
Piquet, Nelson, 102
Pitt, Dirk, 49
Pompidou, Georges, 12
Pontiac Grand Prix, 200
Pope John Paul II, 150
Pope Pius XII, 46
Porsche 911 and 912, 72
Porsche, 123
President Chirac, 12
President Mubarak, 23
President Tito, 23
Presley, Elvis, 62, 63, 192, 200
Prince Bernard of Holland, 84
Prince Rainier of Monaco, 44
Prince Talal al Saoud, 24
Princess Margaret, 24
Putin, Vladimir, 32
Queen Elizabeth, 12, 19, 24
Radford Bentley Mk VI Countryman, 144, 145
Radford Mini, 144
Radford, Harold, 144, 160
Range Rover, 160
Rat Pack, 70
Reed, Oliver, 194
Reliant Scimitar GTE, 156
Ricart, Don Wilfrido, 78
Rivolta, Renzo, 105, 119, 164
Rockefeller, Nelson, 46, 86
Rogers, Kenny, 200
Rolls-Royce, 7, 11, 23, 42, 50, 63, 173, 183,
189
Rolls-Royce Camargue, 198, 199
Rolls-Royce Phantom III, 41, 66, 67
Rolls-Royce Phantom IV, 24, 25
Rolls-Royce Phantom VI, 26, 27
Rolls-Royce Safari, 144
Rolls-Royce Silver Cloud, 27, 144
Rover-BRM Gas Turbine Racer, 167
Saatchi, Charles, 175

Schroeder, Gerhard, 23
Schumacher, Michael, 136
Schwarzenegger, Arnie, 184
Sellers, Peter, 93, 94
Silver Cloud II (Rolls-Royce), 27
Silver Cloud Saloon (Rolls-Royce), 144
Sinatra, Frank, 63, 70
Society of Motor Manufacturers and Traders, 27
Sodomka, 36
Sports Car Club of America, 116
Stalin, Joseph, 36
Starr, Ringo, 91
Steele, Tommy, 184
Stevens, Brook, 184
Stevens, Peter, 127
Studebaker, 184
Stutz Blackhawk, 200, 201
Sultan of Brunei, 143, 200
Superamerica S1, 2 & 3 (Ferrari), 84, 85, 89
Swiss Jensen, 176
Tatra 613 Limousine, 28, 29
Tatra T600 Cabrio, 36, 37
Tatra, 59
Tavistock, Lord and Lady, 202
Taylor, Elizabeth, 197
Tjaarda, Tom, 175
Tokyo Motor Show, 39
Touring of Milan, 172
Towns, William, 167, 202
Toyota 2000GT, 110, 111
Toyota Crown, 110
Vanden Plas 3-litre Princess Countryman, 141
Vanden Plas Estates, 146, 147
Vauxhall Cresta Friary, 146
Vignale, 98
Villa d'Este, 156
Volkswagen, 132
Warner, Jack, 64
Wilhelm II, Kaiser, 20
World War II, 41, 50, 59, 90
Wright, Frank Lloyd, 100
Yeltsin, Boris, 32
Zagato, Adrea, 114
ZIL 111, 30, 31
ZIL 114-117, 32, 33
ZIL 4014, 32
ZIL, 7, 16
ZIS (Zavod Imieni Stalina), 30

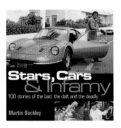

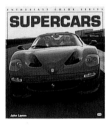

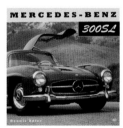